COGNITIVE THERAPY

COGNITIVE THERAPY

BASIC PRINCIPLES AND APPLICATIONS

ROBERT L. LEAHY, PH.D.

JASON ARONSON INC.
Northvale, New Jersey
London

This book was set in 11 pt. Cheltenham by TechType of Ramsey, New Jersey and printed and bound by Book-mart Press of North Bergen, New Jersey.

Library of Congress Cataloging-in-Publication Data

Leahy, Robert L.
    Cognitive therapy : basic principles and applications / Robert L. Leahy.
        p. cm.
    Includes bibliographical references and index.
    ISBN 1-56821-850-8 (hc : alk. paper)
    1. Cognitive therapy. 2. Cognitive therapy—Case studies.
I. Title.
RC489.C63L38   1996
616.89′142—dc20   96-11691

Manufactured in the United States of America. Jason Aronson Inc. offers books and cassettes. For information and catalog write to Jason Aronson Inc., 230 Livingston Street, Northvale, New Jersey 07647.

for Helen

Contents

PART III   SPECIFIC APPLICATIONS

PREFACE

In writing a book on cognitive therapy, I have had to examine the underlying assumptions and models in carrying out therapy. This has been an interesting experience because it reveals how structured, rational, *and demanding* cognitive therapy really is. After all, as therapists we are expected to be active, constantly engaging and challenging the patient. To describe the way in which the cognitive therapist continually conceptualizes cases, and plans and carries out interventions makes one aware of the proactive and challenging nature of this kind of approach.

My own route to becoming a cognitive therapist was quite circuitous. I began my work in clinical psychology with a great reverence for classical psychoanalytic theory. I was impressed with the significant contribution of Freud and his early group and with the work of Federn, Hartmann, Schafer, Kris, and Rapaport. But as I explored psychoanalytic diagnosis, treatment, and theory I became increasingly dissatisfied with the slow and often unclear nature of progress. I might have turned to behavior therapy, but at that time it seemed limited and overly simplistic. My impatience even motivated me to pursue developmental research on social cognition and self-image since I believed that these factors affected the development of psychopathology.

Finally, in the late 1970s I came across the work of Aaron Beck. His writings on cognitive therapy seemed to integrate well with the cognitive revolution in developmental and social psychology. I found that the cognitive approach seemed to offer a rational, empirically based, active, and practical approach to solving problems. Consequently, I took a break from academic and social-developmental psychology to go to the Center for Cognitive Therapy at the University of Pennsylvania and work with Beck. Intellectually, this was the single most important decision of my life.

One advantage in writing a book is that you have the opportunity to thank the people who have helped you along the way. I wish to thank Aaron "Tim" Beck, the founder of cognitive therapy, for the opportunity to work with him at the Center for Cognitive Therapy and for his continued support and encouragement over the last twelve years. More than that of anyone else in my lifetime, Tim Beck's work has dramatically changed the nature of the field of psychotherapy. I am even more impressed with the fact that his earlier contributions were made at a time when the environment was quite unfriendly to this approach—yet he persevered. We are all deeply grateful to Tim for his continuing significant contribution to the field.

I also wish to thank David Burns for his excellent supervision during the early years of my career and his support over the last decade. David's intelligence, energy, humor, and insight have been invaluable to me professionally and personally. In addition, my colleagues at the American Institute for Cognitive Therapy in New York and at Cornell University

Medical College have been important sources of ideas and stimulation. In particular, I wish to thank Stephen Holland who has been an excellent colleague over the last five years. My earlier supervisors in cognitive therapy at the Center for Cognitive Therapy—Art Freeman, Jeff Young, Bob Berchick, and Norm Epstein—were important influences on my thinking. My earlier supervisors in behavior therapy—Steve Gordon, Eve Feindler and Bob McMahon—were essential in my understanding of behavior therapy principles.

Of course, our patients are our ultimate teachers. Perhaps Beck says it best when he reminds us not to assume that we know what the patient thinks: "Ask them!" I have found that the best incentive in this work is to think of the patient as our collaborator in discovering the cause and cure of the problem.

And, of course, my greatest appreciation is for my wife, Helen, who has always been the voice of optimism and excellent humor. She has always encouraged me in my work even at the times when I was most irrational. Helen's work as a theatrical producer and director and my work as a psychologist help me recognize that we both study the same phenomena—but perhaps she does it with more *panache*. It is with deep pleasure and gratitude that I dedicate this book to her.

1

INTRODUCTION

During the last fifteen years there has been a dramatic change in the provision of therapeutic services in the United States. On one hand, there is increasing awareness of the ubiquity of depression, anxiety, substance abuse, and marital conflict, as well as an increasing awareness of childhood disorders. National surveys of adult disorders reveal that 50 percent of that population will have experienced a psychiatric disorder sometime during their lifetime and, that among those who have one disorder, about 85 percent have more than one diagnosable disorder. Governmental and interest groups concerned with making the public aware of the general pervasiveness of these problems have established "awareness days" and have helped reduce the stigmatization of seeking treatment.

Along with the growing awareness and acceptance of the pervasiveness of psychiatric problems is a decreasing willingness of insurance carriers to provide financial support for longer-term individual psychotherapy. In many states, the average number of patient–therapist sessions is fewer than five, with some managed care companies trying to reduce contact hours even more. Hospitalization of patients has been drastically reduced by changes in managed care and Medicare, placing additional pressure on the practitioner for interventions that may be applied rapidly. Further pressure comes from the "medicalizing" of depression and anxiety, with optimistic claims by physicians and drug companies of the efficacy of inexpensive pharmacological treatments for a variety of disorders. However, the pharmacological treatment of some disorders (such as panic or obsessive-compulsive disorder) has mixed results: whereas the medications may suppress symptoms, the discontinuation of medication results in a substantial rebound of symptoms.

Psychiatric patients view themselves in a more assertive role today; they shop around for cost-effective treatments that make sense to them, and they want to know how the specific treatment advocated by a practitioner will be relevant to their specific problem. One could say that consumers of psychotherapy are demanding more accountability from practitioners who would be wise to address these inquiries without viewing them as resistance.

To add to the pressure of the individual practitioner interested in providing psychotherapy, there is a proliferation of therapists in the marketplace, each adding to the competition and many claiming special knowledge and techniques with proven (or unproven) efficacy. As a result, the therapy consumer is often left in a quandary as to what therapy is and how it is relevant to his problem.

As a therapist with years of experience in dealing with patients, I recognize that no approach is a panacea, including cognitive-behavior therapy (CBT).[1] My observation is that as

---

[1]Throughout this book, cognitive-behavior therapy (CBT) and cog-

therapists become more experienced they often become more eclectic, recognizing the value of integrating a variety of approaches. Given the current real-world constraints, many therapists will find that they benefit considerably in helping their patients by integrating CBT into their practice. However, I do not view this as precluding further work with patients in psychodynamic therapy. For example, it is not uncommon for a patient currently in psychodynamic therapy to be referred for CBT for a specific problem—panic, OCD (obsessive-compulsive disorder), or social phobia. The clinician who can draw on skills from CBT may be able to provide additional benefits to his or her patient.

This book was written for the practitioner with little or no background in cognitive therapy. The reader may use it as an introduction to an approach that he or she may wish to follow in a focused way (that is as "a cognitive-behavior therapist") or, more likely, integrate these techniques and ideas into a more eclectic practice. I have noticed with interest how many cognitive therapists who have distinguished themselves in the field actually incorporate conceptualizations from other theoretical models, such as object relations, family systems, biological models, Piagetian, Bowlbian, and psychodynamic theory. I hope that this book will be of interest to like-minded therapists open to new ideas and methods that may enhance their effectiveness.

WHICH COGNITIVE-BEHAVIOR THERAPY?

There is no one cognitive therapy—just as there is no one psychodynamic therapy. Cognitive-behavior therapy includes Beck's model, Rehm's self-control model, Meichenbaum's self-

---

nitive therapy will be used interchangeably. Preference is given to the latter term, since it is more frequently used in current literature on Beck's model.

instructional training, Mahoney's social-constructivism, as well as models drawing upon emotional expression and "inner wounded child." Behavioral models vary considerably, with some emphasizing reinforcement contingencies, social exchange, Pavlovian factors, or mental imagery.

A further development in the last decade has been the specialization of cognitive models. For example, Beck's treatment of depression differs from Clark's cognitive therapy of panic. Specialized treatments abound in the adult area—for example, treatment models for substance abuse, bulimia, borderline personality, anger, social phobia, generalized anxiety, and a variety of personality disorders. There are few problems that are not addressed by cognitive therapy.

Rather than cover every possible model, I have limited my discussion to Beckian cognitive therapy for depression and other behavioral models for OCD and panic. In addition, I have attempted to cover the cognitive approach to relationship conflict and I have presented a case conceptualization of a patient with both Axis I (depression and anxiety) and Axis II (obsessive and narcissistic) features. The interested reader may find that the ideas set forth in this book will be useful in following up on more specialized treatments for other problems.

Although I recognize that sexist language is to be avoided, I feel awkward using "he/she" throughout. The reader should recognize that my choice in using "he" is to avoid an awkward style. Gender is meant to be neutral when these pronouns are used. I have altered the identifying information of patients discussed here so that their anonymity and privacy are protected.

THE PLAN

The purpose here is to provide the practitioner with a useful manual for evaluating and treating a variety of psychiatric disorders using cognitive therapy. My intention is to make the book user-friendly so that the practitioner with little or no background in cognitive therapy (or jargon) may quickly gain some familiarity with the ideas and interventions of this approach. I have kept at a minimum any discussion of research or theoretical controversies of interest to a smaller segment of people.

In the section on "General Theory" I have outlined some of the historical aspects of philosophy and psychology that led to the development of cognitive therapy. I have also provided a general description of Beck's cognitive model of psychopathology, which should serve as a foundation for understanding other sections of this book. In addition, I review some of the common ideas of CBT—for example, its short-term, structured, present-orientation, problem-solving focus. In the section on "Assessment and Interventions" I examine the more important behavioral and cognitive principles and interventions that serve as the basis of the many interventions described throughout this book. In the section on "Specific Applications" I have focused on three areas of considerable interest to clinicians—depression, anxiety, and marital (or couples) therapy. In addition, I provide a description of case conceptualization in treating a patient with complicated problems resulting from developmental trauma and personality disorder. Furthermore, I review some of the issues of transference and countertransference.

Rather than draw comparisons between this approach and other therapeutic models, I have chosen—for the sake of brevity and clarity—to leave those comparisons to the reader. I am less interested in demonstrating the preferability of one approach over others, for I would agree with the axiom that "all have won and all deserve prizes."

I

GENERAL THEORY

2

HISTORICAL CONTEXT OF COGNITIVE THERAPY

PHILOSOPHICAL PRECURSORS

The fundamentals of cognitive therapy have been around since the ancient Greeks. The idea that our perceptions determine the reality we experience was clearly a focus of Plato's idealism. In the classic story, known as "Plato's Cave," Socrates describes how a group of men who are chained in a cave facing a wall observe shadows dancing across the wall in front of them. They had never known that these shadows are due to figures near the entrance to the cave moving behind them in front of a candle. To these men, the shadows are reality. One day one of the men turns around and sees that there are figures moving behind him casting their shadows. From that day on, the reality of the shadows no longer exists. Reality is now defined as the figures that one sees outside the cave. We might view cognitive therapy as the attempt to get the patient to unchain himself and see outside the cave.

Plato's philosophy was the search for ideal forms or qualities—whether Socrates spoke of geometry, love, justice, or political structure. The Platonists believed that these ideal forms were innate to the human mind and that one only needed to "educate" (that is, draw it out of the mind) through questioning. Truth and reality were entirely determined by Platonic ideals. Socrates attempted to demonstrate this in one of the dialogues by asking an uneducated man a series of directed questions about the principles of geometry. From these questions and answers Socrates demonstrated that the ideals of geometry were already there and had only to be extracted through questioning (Cornford 1957).

The idea that "reality is determined by cognition" has a long history in Western philosophy. For example, Kant's (1782/1988) philosophy of mind was based on the view that reality is never directly knowable, but rather is "known" through "categories of thinking." Some of these categories are viewed as innate—prior to experience: for example, categories of quantity, intensity, cause and effect. According to Kant, all knowledge was based on the categories (which today we would call *schemas*). Consequently, reality was never directly knowable—we could only know the schemas.

British empiricists rejected Kant's idea of innate categories and argued that our understanding of reality was simply a matter of associations of events. Thus, if we saw that two events occurred together we might correctly or incorrectly conclude that one was a cause of the other. Empiricists like Hume and Bentham were more interested in examining the factors that led to association and learning—such as the importance of reward or punishment—and less concerned with understanding the specific categories. The importance of empiricism is that the emphasis changed from knowing the universal categories (such as Plato or Kant would have argued), to examining how in the real world we came to associate one stimulus with another or viewed one factor as a cause of another. Since empiricism argued that knowledge is somewhat arbitrarily based on experience, and argued against universal categories, it followed that *knowledge* was precisely in one's point of view. Thus, knowledge became *relativistic* just as moral rules became relativistic. Cognitive therapy is based on a model that cognition and perception may often be based on arbitrarily associated events and that moral rules are individual constructions (rather than universal ideals). Thus, the early founder of cognitive therapy, George Kelly (1955) might say, "That is *your construction of reality*," as if all constructions of reality are on equal footing.

The emphasis on how we experience the world, rather than the emphasis on universal innate categories, gave rise to phenomenological theories of knowledge (Husserl 1960). The phenomenologist is less interested in what reality really is and more interested in how reality is experienced, that is, the "phenomenal experience." Cognitive therapy is derived from this tradition. Although the therapist may assist the patient in testing his cognitions against reality, there is considerable emphasis on the subjective experience of the patient.

The philosophical traditions of examining how the individual constructs reality and how subjective experience is a valid subject of inquiry are the cornerstones of cognitive therapy. One could say that cognitive theory is derived from both the empiricism of the British associationists and the subjectivism of the phenomenological school. These traditions are integrated in what I would call *dynamic structuralism*, that is, the recognition that the structures of experience (schemas) are continuously modified by the individual's interactions with reality.

In a sense, the cognitive therapist assists the patient in "deconstructing" his experience. Just as the deconstructionists might argue that the meaning of a text is in the reader (Derrida

1973), the cognitive therapist assists the patient in recognizing that the meaning of experience is in the perceiver. However, unlike the deconstructionists who seem to imply that reality is unknowable, the cognitive therapist has a more optimistic view—that is, the perceiver's (patient's) beliefs can be tested against reality. Cognitive theorists are not empirical nihilists like the deconstructionists; rather, we see ourselves as structural empiricists. This implies that the structures of knowledge—the patient's schemas—may be tested in the real world.

DEVELOPMENTS IN CLINICAL PSYCHOLOGY

Much of psychology prior to the 1970s was dominated by psychoanalytic theory and learning theory. The "cognitive revolution" was slow in development and seemed to come through the back door into mainstream psychology. In psychodynamic theory, there was an increasing emphasis on ego functioning as opposed to drive theory. Heinz Hartmann (1939/1958) proposed that the ego is "preadaptive," that is, the ego's ability to recognize and process reality was partly initially independent of drive. David Shapiro's (1965) work on "neurotic styles" indicated that different personality types had different styles of experiencing reality. The emphasis in Shapiro's writing was to describe the phenomenology of these different styles of thinking. Similarly, Horney's (1945, 1950) and Sullivan's (1953) descriptions of the patient's ego functioning, somewhat removed from the psychic energy model of the earlier Freud, influenced Beck's thinking (Thase and Beck 1993).

George Kelly's (1955) *Psychology of Personal Constructs* proposed a theory of psychopathology based entirely on cognitive processing. Kelly argued that anxiety, depression, anger, and paranoia were consequences of the individual's construction of reality. Kelly's use of "constructs" is precisely what contemporary theorists describe as schemas. Kelly suggested that people have idiosyncratic constructs that are bipolar. For example, one individual might view events through the construct "strong," but claim that the opposite of strong is "feminine." Another person might claim that the opposite of strong is "helpless." Kelly proposed that individuals differed in the content of their constructs, the degree to which their constructs were open to disconfirmation, and the degree to which information might be assimilated by a construct. Individuals also differed in the complexity and differentiation of their personal constructs. Kelly introduced the idea of *constructive alternativism*, which proposes that individuals differ in their ability to project alternatives or options. Constructive alternativism became an important intervention in Beck's (1987) theory of overcoming hopelessness. Specifically, the hopeless patient is assisted in constructing alternatives to his problems, linking him to potential action.

Kelly's work had more influence on British than on American psychology, probably because of the domination of clinical psychology by psychodynamic and Rogerian theorists who viewed his model as overly intellectualized and not adequately focused on motivation and unconscious processes. Furthermore, Kelly's style of writing is demanding and philosophically oriented, making it less appealing to the reader. However, I would suggest that contemporary cognitive therapists would be well served to read Kelly.

Albert Ellis's *rational emotive therapy*, developed in the 1960s, was an important precursor to Beck's work and the cognitive revolution. Ellis, originally a psychoanalytically oriented sex and marriage therapist, proposed that pathology was entirely due to the irrational distortions of "shoulds"; ("I should be as successful as everyone," or "I should be liked by everyone"); "awfulizing" ("It's awful that I don't succeed"); and low frustration tolerance ("I can't stand waiting"). Ellis proved to be a prolific author, generating books on marriage, sex, substance abuse, procrastination, and a range of other topics for both popular and professional audiences (Ellis 1962, 1971, 1973, 1985, Ellis and Grieger 1977).

STRUCTURE AND DEVELOPMENT

The 1970s witnessed a veritable cognitive revolution in psychology. Increasing importance was placed on the study of how people processed information and the effect of categories on attention and memory. In developmental psychology, Jean Piaget's structural theory of child cognition gained considerable popularity, even though his influence on European psychology had been strong since the 1930s. Piaget (1954, 1965, 1970 and Furth 1969) emphasized that it was more important to identify and describe *qualitative* stages of thinking rather than simply *errors* in thinking. Influenced by Kant's model of innate categories, Piaget attempted to show Kant's error in assuming these categories to be innate. Piaget demonstrated how categories such as number, quantity, volume, and space developed through qualitative stages. Just as Piaget studied the idiosyncratic ideas of children of different ages, Beck (1976, Beck et al. 1979, Thase and Beck 1993) delineated the idiosyncratic ideas of people who were depressed, anxious, or angry. Both Piaget and Beck have advanced *structural theories* (see Leahy 1995) that focus on the systematic structure or logic of thinking rather than on whether the individual (child or patient) is erroneous in his thinking. Thus, the "growth of thinking" is described by structuralists in terms of the kinds of theories that individuals have, rather than simply their acquisition of information that is stored in memory as a copy of reality.

The emphasis on the *structure of thinking* rather than simply the content of information is reflected in work on *categorical perception*. For example, researchers on infant perception and cross-cultural cognition demonstrated that early perception is categorical—that is, infants will treat a range of stimuli as belonging to the same perceptual category even though the visual or auditory stimuli show considerable variation. For example, infants categorize color into specific groups, treating all members of the group as similar even though they differ in wavelength. Memory is also determined by categorical "fit." Even during infancy, children more easily recall wavelengths that are more representative of a category (e.g., a "good blue"), than wavelengths on the fuzzy boundary of a color category. Similar categorical perception was demonstrated for sound, speech, and figures (see Bornstein 1979, Rosch 1973).

Developmental researchers in the 1970s and through the 1980s demonstrated the ubiquity of categorization, its innate and cross-cultural qualities, and its substantial effect on recognition and recall. This work appeared to contradict simple learning-theory models of "associationism," that is, that all stimuli are equally associable. Categories seemed to preempt simple stimulus-response links. Memory was determined by categories—a concept that found its way into social psychology in the work on schematic processing.

The emphasis on innate categories (or at least on predisposition to structure reality in specific ways) was especially important in linguistic or developmental linguistic theory. Noam Chomsky's important critique of Skinner's *Verbal Behavior* (1957), demonstrated the futility of a simple learning model of language. According to Chomsky (1968), language is too complex and too universally similar to be learned by simple reinforcement. In fact, language is so complex that adult human experts on language are unable to write comprehensive rules for language acquisition. Consequently, Chomsky, in his books

Aspects of a Theory of Syntax (1965) and *Language and Mind* (1968), proposed that all human infants are equipped with the ability to learn language, an ability that psychologists referred to as *language acquisition device* (LAD). This LAD is similar to Platonic ideals or Kant's *synthetic a priori* (innate categories of knowledge). Thus, humans are born with a theory of what language will look like. Humans are language learners and therefore, according to Chomsky, language acquisition is not arbitrary but rather constrained by the structure of human knowing. One might argue that Chomsky's psycholinguistics was the most truly structural theory of the 1970s.

COGNITIVE-SOCIAL PSYCHOLOGY

Social psychology in the 1970s increasingly became cognitive-social psychology. Researchers became interested in the cognitive processes involved in impression-formation, decision-making, self-perception, motivation, and memory. Information-processing models became popular in describing, for example, how people weighed information in forming impressions about others. Of particular relevance to the development of Beck's cognitive theory was new research on schematic processing in memory and research on attribution theory.

Schematic/Semantic Memory

Earlier models of memory were based on the idea that memory was a copy of reality, with decay of memory determined by factors such as initial repetition or time elapsed. In contrast, schematic models of memory proposed that people form categories or schemas that guide attention and memory. For example, in one study two groups of subjects read passages about a person who was either "extroverted" or "introverted." Subsequently, both groups were given the same passage to read about the person and then asked to recall what they had read. Memory was schema-consistent. Subjects who were told that the person was extroverted not only recalled more information consistent with that attribute, but they also *falsely recalled* information consistent with the schema: that is, they made up information consistent with the view that the person was extroverted. In another study the schema was presented *after* the subjects were asked to read a passage about a woman. One group was told that the woman was a lesbian; the other group was not given this information. Subjects in the lesbian-schema group falsely recalled more information consistent with the idea that the woman was a lesbian.

Numerous studies since then have shown that schemas can have a dramatic effect on memory. Loftus (1980, Loftus and Ketcham 1995) has shown that subjects who were told that they were lost in a mall when they were younger actually came to believe that they were lost and made up stories consistent with this belief. Loftus has argued that her research casts doubt on the *repressed memory* phenomena that are the foundation of claims about childhood abuse. In any case, the foregoing studies are an important component of the research and theoretical foundation of cognitive theory, demonstrating that schemas direct memory. When we discuss Beck's cognitive theory, we will see how important schemas are in determining the development and maintenance of depression and anxiety.

Attribution Theory

Fritz Heider was the forerunner of contemporary cognitive-social psychology, interested in what he called *naive psychology,* or how the average person formed psychological concepts such as intention and motivation or how people

explained behavior. Heider's work (1958) had considerable influence on attribution theory, which is concerned with how
individuals use information to form impressions of dispositions,
intentions, and abilities (Jones and Davis 1965, Kelley 1967,
Weiner 1974). Of particular relevance to cognitive theory is
Weiner's attribution cube. According to Weiner, success with a
task can be attributed to internal factors (ability or effort) and
external factors (task difficulty or luck). Furthermore, these
attributions refer to whether the cause is stable (ability or task
difficulty) or unstable (effort or luck). (See Table 1–1.)

Weiner's model had considerable influence on the study and
the perception of motivation. He has recently extended his
work (1995) to identify how concepts of personal responsibility
are related to the attribution process.

Weiner's work was of considerable importance to the development of Seligman's cognitive model of depression
(Abramson et al. 1978). Seligman's (1975) earlier model of
depression proposed that depression is a consequence of the
individual's perception that behavior and outcomes are unre-
lated (non-contingent): that is, no matter how hard I work, it
will have no effect on rewards or punishments. With the
perception of non-contingency, the individual shows decreased behavior, motivation, and ability to learn (all signs of
depression). As elegant, simple, and research-based as this
model was, it soon became apparent that the model needed
significant modification.

Studies by Carol Dweck (Dweck and Goetz 1978) on helplessness in children demonstrated that children who often

Table 1–1. Weiner's Attribution Cube

	Internal	External
Stable	Ability	Task Difficulty
Unstable	Effort	Luck

gave up when they failed would verbalize attributions such as, "I must not be good at this" and "These puzzles are too hard for me" (both *stable attributions for failure*). Consequently, if they believed that their failure was due to something unchangeable, it made sense to give up. In one study, Dweck attempted to modify the explanations that children gave for their failure. One group was given 100 percent success experiences on puzzles, whereas another group was given the experience of occasionally failing. However, when they failed, the researcher would say, "You didn't try hard enough" (an internal, unstable attribution). In the next phase of the study, subjects were given success experiences followed by failure. The attribution-training group actually improved following failure, whereas the reward group showed substantial decrements in performance.

A second question that the earlier helplessness model could not handle is why individuals confronting non-contingency would become self-critical. It might make sense that their performance would decrease, but the model did not adequately explain changes in self-criticism (or individual differences in self-criticism).

Consequently, Seligman and his colleagues (Abramson, et al. 1978) turned to Weiner's attribution cube to develop a cognitive model of depression (a model I believe to be consistent with Beck's cognitive model). According to the *reformulated model*, depression is a consequence of the belief that failure is due to a stable and internal factor (lack of ability) that is generalized beyond the immediate task for behavior and is viewed by the individual as important (Abramson et al. 1978). Since the publication of the reformulated model of depression, Abramson and her colleagues have made significant advances in developing a hopelessness model of depression based on attribution theory. These developments in clinical psychology were clearly derivative of the importantadvances in cognitive social psychology, reflecting how cognitive therapy then, as now, was influenced by academic research.

BECK'S INITIAL DISCOVERIES ON DEPRESSION

Aaron T. Beck, founder of cognitive therapy, was trained in a traditional medical model of psychoanalysis. Educated at Yale Medical School and the Psychoanalytic Institute of Philadelphia, Beck was interested in testing the Freudian view that depression is due to anger turned inward. Beck hypothesized that the dreams of depressed individuals should be replete with themes of anger and retaliation, since their ego defenses against anger would be compromised during sleep. Contrary to his expectations, Beck found that the dreams of depressed patients were characterized by the same themes of loss, emptiness, and failure as their conscious reports during therapy sessions. Beck decided to examine the conscious spontaneous verbalizations of patients during psychoanalysis for these themes of loss and failure. He noted that depression seemed to be characterized by a negative bias in viewing reality and referred to it as the *negative triad*—that is, a negative view of self, experience, and the future. Thus, depressed patients believed they were failures, that experience was without reward, and that the future looked bleak. Further, Beck noted that during sessions, patients would often verbalize their negativity with specific cognitive distortions that he labeled *automatic thoughts* because they were conscious thoughts that came spontaneously and seemed plausible and true to the patients. These automatic thoughts were the basis of the depressive style of thinking which, for Beck, became the major focus of inquiry and change. Therapy in this new model would focus on modifying automatic thoughts and testing them against reality. Consequently, his model moved from the emphasis on unconscious conflict and hydraulic energies to a model of rational and empirical testing.

Beck's model, which I will discuss in greater detail in the next chapter, was being developed during the 1960s and 1970s and continues to develop today. During this period there were parallel developments in structural psychology (Piaget, cognitive social psychology, Kelly's psychology of personal constructs). However, the early years for Beck were years in which he moved against the mainstream of psychoanalytic thinking. Much to his credit, he did not abandon the validity of his early observations on depression and made important contributions to the cognitive model of psychopathology.

THE CURRENT CONTEXT

Although cognitive therapy was initially used for depression, it has enjoyed considerable success during the past decade for a variety of other disorders. There are now effective cognitive therapy models for treating panic disorder (Beck et al. 1986, Clark 1986), generalized anxiety (Beck et al. 1985), social phobia (Clark and Wells 1995), dysthymia (Mercier 1993), childhood depression and anger (Novaco, 1978), marital conflict (Baucom and Epstein 1990), substance abuse (Beck et al. 1993), schizophrenia (Alford and Correia 1994), bipolar disorder, borderline personality (Layden et al. 1993) and a variety of other personality disorders (Beck et al. 1990).

The current context of clinical practice in the United States appears to be moving toward an eclecticism in which most therapists incorporate some cognitive principles in their work (Alford and Beck in press, Alford and Norcross 1991). For the remainder of this book I will describe the cognitive therapy model and how it is applied to three areas—depression, anxiety, and marital conflict. The reader is encouraged to read more detailed treatment manuals and books on all of these and other disorders now treated with cognitive therapy. In addition, case studies of a variety of disorders using cognitive therapy may be found in *Casebook in Cognitive Therapy* (in press) edited by the author.

3

COGNITIVE MODEL OF PSYCHOPATHOLOGY

GENERAL PRINCIPLES OF THE COGNITIVE MODEL

As indicated in the previous chapter, there are many cognitive models we could discuss: for example, the work of Ellis, Meichenbaum, Mahoney, Rehm, and others. I have chosen to focus on Beck's work because I view his model of psychopathology as far more comprehensive and precise than other models and because there is considerably more research supporting the efficacy of the cognitive model. Furthermore, Beck's theoretical position allows us to integrate other cognitive models in a manner that preserves the integrity of all (see Alford and Beck [in press] for an excellent discussion of cognitive theory and the integration of other models).

Beck's cognitive model of emotional disorders has a number of common general principles. Although the conceptualization

of various disorders and their treatment varies—there is no
one treatment for all disorders—one can identify common
features of the Beckian model. The central importance of
cognition, schematic content, cognitive bias, and compensation—all of which will be explained later—provides the cognitive model with a general theoretical framework. It is important to understand this general framework, since the
application of cognitive therapy necessitates an understanding
of cognitive assessment and some key terms and concepts.

Cognitive Distortions

Although the term is used to describe frequent errors in
thinking associated with negative affect, Beck has always
recognized that many negative thoughts that patients have
may also be true. For example, the patient who predicts that
he will be rejected at an interview (fortune telling) may indeed
be correct. One could argue, however, that depressed, anxious, or angry individuals have cognitive biases that are sometimes correct and sometimes not.

This is an important point to make. Some patients (and
therapists) may incorrectly believe that cognitive therapy is
simply naive optimism. A French patient of mine commented
that he hoped that cognitive therapy was not simply Pangloss
in Voltaire's *Candide ("The Optimist")* arguing that this was
"the best of all possible worlds." Indeed, the experienced
therapist knows that in real life many negative thoughts are
true. In fact, some patients may suffer more because of their
inability to correctly diagnose or prepare for negative events.
Cognitive therapy is the *power of realistic thinking, not the
power of positive thinking.*

Schemas

The cognitive model identifies three levels of cognitive distortion or bias. At the deepest or most central level are the

individual's schemas. Schemas are the concepts the patient habitually uses in viewing reality. These biases direct his focus and retrieval of information. Typical negative schemas are: rejection, abandonment, control, uniqueness, and unrelenting standards.

For example, a person with the negative schema of rejection will tend to focus on any sign that she is being rejected. Another person with the negative schema of abandonment will focus on any evidence that he has been abandoned. Thus, schemas are defined by the *specific bias of their content,* are usually formed during early childhood, and selectively focus information processing.

Maladaptive Assumptions

The second level of cognitive distortion is the maladaptive assumption or set of rules that the person uses to guide and evaluate his own and others' behavior. They are usually stated as: "I should do . . ." or "If I do x, then y will follow," or "I must have . . ." Examples of these assumptions or rules are: "People will reject me if they really get to know me," "I have to control all of my feelings all of the time," "I have to win everyone's approval to be worthwhile," "I should never let anyone control me," "I need to be better than everyone," or "I need to do a perfect job in order to prove that I'm not a failure."

Beck and colleagues (1990) have proposed that these maladaptive assumptions are attempts to cope with the negativity of the negative schemas. For example, imagine if an individual has the negative schema "I am unlovable." He might develop assumptions or rules that he believes will help him cope with his "unlovability." This might include trying to be excessively pleasing: "If I am very pleasing to others and put their needs first, then they will love me." Another way in which the individual copes is to avoid any challenge to himself: "If I get involved with people, then they will see that I am really unlovable. Therefore, I should avoid intimacy." Thus, the cognitive model proposes that individuals will compensate for or avoid their negative schemas. We will describe this when we discuss personality disorders and in a later chapter on case conceptualization.

Automatic Thoughts

The third and most immediately accessible level of cognitive distortion involves automatic thoughts. These are thoughts (or even images) that come to the individual spontaneously and are associated with negative affect. They seem plausible and are often left unexamined. Beck has categorized these typical thought patterns into *distortions* (although all three levels may be viewed as biases that are sometimes distortions). Typical examples of automatic thought distortions are: "It's terrible to be rejected" (catastrophizing); "I'm a failure" (mislabeling); "I am always messing up" (dichotomous thinking); and "I will be rejected" (negative prediction or fortune telling). Example:

> A highly successful executive had the following automatic thoughts: "I will make a fool of myself at the next meeting" (fortune telling) and "People don't think I am competent" (mind reading). He claimed that "If other people think I am incompetent, then I am incompetent" (maladaptive assumption). His underlying negative schema about himself was "I am incompetent." He attempted to cope with his schema of being incompetent by being a workaholic and by constantly trying to please others. Regardless of his coping style and his obvious success in business, he still had not challenged his negative schema of incompetence.

Content Specificity

The cognitive model of psychopathology proposes that each diagnostic category of pathology may be characterized by its typical negative content. Thus, we can distinguish among different problems (such as anxiety and depression) by examining the specific content or themes of the individual's negative thoughts. Specifically, anxiety focuses on issues of imminent threat while depression focuses on the belief that one has already failed. For example, the following are common emotional disorders and their typical content:

Emotional Disorders

Depression: loss, failure, emptiness
Anxiety: threat, imminent loss and failure, lack of control
Anger: humiliation, insult, threat
Mania: unlimited ability

Personality Disorders

Paranoia: manipulation and defeat by others
Narcissism: special, superior person, deprivation
Dependence: abandonment, helplessness
Avoidance: rejection, negative evaluation, fundamental flaw

This list reveals that there are possible relationships between the content of depression (or anxiety) and the personality disorders. Thus, the dependent personality becomes anxious or depressed over possible losses in the domain of personal relationships because such losses activate feelings of helplessness. In contrast, the paranoid becomes anxious or angry over being manipulated or dominated by others. Consider the following examples:

Depression: A depressed woman believed she was a failure because she had fallen behind in school. She thought she

would never be able to achieve any success because she had
a permanent flaw.

Anxiety: A socially phobic man believed others could see he
was anxious and as a result they would think he was weak.

Narcissism: A highly narcissistic man would berate his limo
driver with statements such as: "Do you know who I am?
Who do you think you are that you can treat me this way?"

Cognitive Vulnerability

The cognitive model proposes that individuals differ in their
vulnerability to cognitive distortion and consequent emotional
disorder. One can view individual differences in terms of prior
or early maladaptive schemas and underlying maladaptive
assumptions. For example, although many patients in therapy
or on antidepressant medication show remission of depression, those patients whose maladaptive assumptions and
schemas remain unchanged remain vulnerable to relapse.
These schemas and assumptions may become latent rather
than permanently modified during remission, leaving the patient with the incorrect belief that he is cured.

Another aspect of cognitive vulnerability reveals that individuals differ in what I would call the structural resistance of
their schemas and assumptions. Consider the following. We
are all familiar with people in our lives who maintain certain
beliefs no matter what evidence or logic to the contrary we
present. Similarly, schemas and assumptions may differ in
terms of being impermeable, difficult to disconfirm, rigid, and
overgeneralized. These structural qualities make it difficult to
modify these cognitions, resulting in their persistence, independent of apparently contradictory events.

An additional view of the vulnerability model is that individuals differ in those issues that arouse depression, anxiety, or
anger. Beck (1987) has identified two general areas of vulner-

ability—*sociotropy* and *autonomy*. (See also Blatt et al. 1979 for a discussion of similar modalities.) The sociotropic individual focuses on acceptance, closeness, dependence, and sharing, whereas the autonomous individual focuses on independent functioning, mobility, choice, and achievement. Thus, life events may have different effects on individuals who differ in sociotropy and autonomy. Some people typically become depressed over their perception of poor achievement, others become depressed because of loneliness and rejection, while still others over both autonomic and sociotropic issues.

Cognitive Diathesis-Stress Model

The cognitive model proposes that these early, maladaptive, and persistent schemas are activated when stressful life events occur. For example, in the termination of an intimate relationship, the dependent personality who maintains schemas of helplessness will become depressed. With the activation of his negative schemas of helplessness, this individual will predict that he cannot take care of himself or achieve happiness without this relationship; he will blame himself for the relationship ending, and he will try to cope with the loss by doing anything to revive the relationship or to find an immediate substitute. The underlying schemas and assumptions are the diathesis or predisposition to respond to various threats with a habitual pattern of thinking and behavior. Stressful life events become stressful by virtue of their relevance to a schema.

THEORY OF DEPRESSION

Negative Triad and Negative Bias

Unlike the earlier psychoanalytic model that views depression as anger turned inward, the cognitive model argues that depression is either a consequence of or is maintained by negative biases in thinking. Specifically, depression involves the negative triad—that is, a negative view of self ("I am a failure"), experience ("This is not enjoyable") and the future ("I will continue to be rejected").

The specific clusters of symptoms of depression have corresponding negative cognitions.

Self-criticism: I'm a failure, worthless, helpless.
Motivation: I don't have any energy. I can't do it.
Indecision: I can't make good decisions. I'll regret it.
Vegetation: I'm not hungry or interested, so I may as well not eat or do anything.
Withdrawal: I'm just a burden. People don't want me around.

A woman who was separated from her husband and contemplating divorce reported her negative thinking: "I ruined the marriage; it's all my fault. I don't have any desire to do anything. I'll be depleted if I try. I don't know what to do with my life. I'm just a depressing burden to my friends so I'm better off not spending time with them."

Information Processing and Depression

Unlike psychodynamic models that emphasize unconscious motivation and unconscious conflicts, the cognitive model stresses biases in information processing as a source of depression. Information processing refers to the manner in which information is selected, focused, recollected, recognized, and evaluated. For example, for the depressive with a negative schema of failure there is a biased selection in the immediate situation of information consistent with failure, a narrowed focus on that information (to the exclusion of disconfirmatory information), a tendency to recall past failures selectively or to recognize signs of failure, and a tendency to evaluate even neutral events as signs of failure. This selectivity of information consistent with the negative schema is known as *schematic processing*.

Consider the following analogies. The software with which this book was written has a *search* function. I can search for all examples in the text of the word *failure*. The search function will ignore *success* (or any other words for that matter). If I were to incorrectly view the search for *failure* as the sole indication of what this book is about, I would conclude that this is a very depressing book. In a similar vein, the depressive person searches out all examples of failure and incorrectly concludes that it is representative of reality. Of course, it is representative of one sampling of reality. It is not that the depressive wants to be depressed. It is simply that he is biased in his information search and selection. Example:

> A man complained of periodic cycles of depression. When he was not depressed, he felt extremely competent and was quite productive in his work. During his depressions, all he could do was focus on any signs of past failure and loss and predict that he was totally unable to get any work done. He believed that he would lose his job because of his inability to perform. Despite these negative predictions, he continued to be successful even though he experienced frequent cycles of depression.

Negative Evaluation

Just as he selectively processes information, the depressive also has an exaggerated evaluation of information. For example, one could ask, "What constitutes a failure?" and, "If you did fail, what would it mean to you?" For many depressives the definition of failure is "less than perfection" resulting in an enormous number of "false positives" (or incorrect evaluations of failure). The answer to the second question on the meaning of failure is similarly exaggerated: "It means that I am a failure," or that "Everyone will reject me." The non-depressed individual is less likely to have perfectionist standards and less likely to view failure at a task as a global, moral, unchanging aspect of the self. Example:

> A highly competitive athlete who had a brief period of playing a professional sport (despite his small size) viewed himself as a failure: "I didn't make it in the pros." Thus, he discounted the huge success he had achieved in high school and college and even being able to play in the pros. Since he had not achieved the highest goal, he discounted whatever achievements he had made.

Cognition, Behavior, and Affect

The cognitive model does not view cognition as always primary to depression. Depression may arise because of biological factors or negative life events (such as divorce, loss of a job, or loss of valued resources). However, once the depression is aroused, there are corresponding or consequent changes in cognition and behavior. The depression is associated with the activation of negative schemas, some of which may be early maladaptive ones that have been dormant or latent for some time. Maladaptive assumptions are activated with their consequent rigidity, globality, and negativity, further aggravating the depression, resulting in affective changes of hopelessness, helplessness, and saddened affect. Because the individual has such a negative view of himself, his capacities to cope, and his future prospects, productive behavior seems pointless. Consequently he withdraws, reduces his productivity, and gives up. This further reduces his chances for reward, deepening the depression.

Other Cognitive Models of Depression

The Beckian model is not inconsistent with other cognitive models of depression. For example, Lewinsohn and colleagues (1985) have advanced what they describe as an integrative model that overlaps considerably with the Beckian cognitive model. They propose that negative life events lead to disruption of important behavior patterns and consequently reductions in positive reinforcements. This results in an increase in aversive experiences leading to increased self-awareness (self-criticism, self-focus, focus on negative mood), which results in dysphoria. The consequence of this is cognitive, behavioral, and emotional negativity, which leads to activation or exacerbation of individual vulnerabilities, which then begins the cycle anew. The Lewinsohn model of treatment places considerable emphasis on increasing positive and decreasing negative behavior and experiences, improving social skills, improving self-reinforcement, training in problem-solving, and intervening in the marital relationship, if necessary (see Lewinsohn and Gotlib 1995).

Rehm's self-control theory (1977, 1990) has been incorporated into the Lewinsohn and colleagues' model, placing emphasis on goal attainment, self-reinforcement, and contingency management. Lewinsohn and colleagues (1984) have developed an excellent Coping With Depression (CWD) course for patients, which can be offered to groups and includes bibliotherapy (reading) as part of its educational format. This cost-effective program for patients has proven to be effective in dealing with depression.

These behavioral models are consistent with the cognitive model, although the latter places more emphasis on the patient's intrapsychic processes and provides a more adequate explanation of why self-criticism is a consequence of depression. Cognitive therapists make use of most if not all of the concepts and interventions advocated by Lewinsohn.

Another cognitive model of depression described in the previous chapter is the *learned helplessness* model advanced by Abramson and colleagues (1978). According to this model, depression is the result of the explanatory style the individual brings to negative events. Depression and self-criticism are the consequence of viewing negative events as due to lack of ability, that others would have done better, and that these negative events will continue and generalize to other events of importance. This model is, of course, consistent with the cognitive model and extends it into the productive realm of empirical research carried out by Seligman, Teasdale, Abramson and their colleagues.

Finally, Nolen-Hoecksema (1987) has proposed that individuals with a ruminative style of thinking are more likely to become depressed than individuals with an instrumental style. Ruminators are more likely to respond to negative events or negative affect by dwelling on how bad they feel, complaining, asking rhetorical questions that have no answers ("Why am I feeling so bad? What's wrong with me?") and general passivity. In contrast, individuals who are resourceful or instrumental respond to negative events or affect by attempting to distract themselves, engaging in productive activity, or taking advice from others to change themselves. Nolen-Hoecksema finds that ruminators are more likely to become depressed, stay depressed longer, have more severe depressions and more frequent relapses. Furthermore, women are more likely than men to be ruminators. Ironically, ruminators report that they focus on their negativity because they believe it will facilitate a solution to their problems.

These various models serve to supplement the more comprehensive model advanced by Beck. For example, cognitive therapy is an active, problem-solving therapy with homework assignments to offset the negative effects of rumination. Because the cognitive therapist helps the patient examine alternative ways of thinking, she may begin to challenge her typical, self-blaming style of thinking. Furthermore, the emphasis in cognitive therapy on pleasurable activities helps provide new challenges to the patient's negative belief that nothing will make her feel better. Finally, as we shall see in the chapters on depression and marital therapy, the patient may be assisted in acquiring a variety of social skills that can help her obtain more rewards in her social environment.

THEORY OF ANXIETY

Biological Value

Beck and colleagues' (1985) theory of anxiety draws upon Beck's earlier (1976) model of anxiety emphasizing the role of cognitive appraisal. Influenced by the ethological and socio-biological models of social behavior (e.g., Wilson 1975), Beck's theory proposes that many of the symptoms of anxiety can be understood as having adaptive value in natural or primitive environments, where humans were vulnerable to attack from predators or other humans. The fact that many of these symptoms are found in many non-human species suggests that there is an adaptive value of these symptoms in natural environments. In this sense, Beck's model of anxiety is a threat model, emerging from cognitive appraisals of external and internal threats to the individual. The symptoms of anxiety are emergency responses to those perceived threats.

For example, the symptoms of mobilization, inhibition, and demobilization that characterize active defense, avoidance of risky behavior, and the collapse response of helplessness were probably adaptive for animals (and humans) confronted with physical threat (Beck et al. 1985). The active defense symptoms—increased hypervigilance, sensitivity to sound, and increased heart rate—may have assisted earlier humans in the fight-or-flight responses. Inhibitory symptoms, for example, blocking of thinking, clouding of consciousness, and muscle rigidity—would prevent the individual from taking too many risks. An example of this inhibitory response is the fear of heights, so that the individual is not be able to move forward toward the edge of the cliff. Demobilization might involve feelings of weakness, fatigue, and/or lowering of blood pressure and heart rate, resulting in collapse or freeze responses. These symptoms of demobilization might result in predators failing to see an immobile individual, thereby conferring adaptive value on humans showing these responses in natural environments (see also Marks 1987 for a discussion of innate fears and their adaptive value).

Beck and Emery (Beck et al. 1985) identify a number of innate patterns or responses that are found across species in response to threat. These include fight, flight, freeze, faint (collapse), retraction, dodging, clinging, calling for help, and other responses, such as blinking, gagging, or coughing. These responses are viewed as having adaptive value, increasing the ability to defend or decreasing the likelihood of being trapped or detected. There are corresponding cognitive implications for the innate patterns one sees in anxiety patients: "I have to get out of here," "I can't move," "What is happening to me?" or "Don't leave me." These cognitive responses further aggravate the anxiety, leading to greater impulse toward the emergency response.

Cognitive Factors in Anxiety

Anxiety is a thinking disorder. According to the cognitive model, it is the result of distortions in information processing. These distortions include hypervigilance, false alarms, loss of objectivity, generalization of danger to other stimuli, catastrophizing, excessive focus on negative outcomes, no tolerance for uncertainty, and lack of habituation (Beck et al. 1985). For example, once anxiety is aroused (or, alternatively, as a cause of anxiety), the individual becomes hypervigilant, looking for any signs of danger or threat. The social phobic looks for signs of rejection, the test-anxious individual looks for signs that he will fail, and the panic disorder patient monitors any signs of arousal. False alarms are a key element in the anxiety disorders, with the individual constantly believing that bad things are about to happen. For example, the panic disorder patient believes that she is about to have a heart attack or go insane, and the social phobic believes that she will make a fool of herself. The obsessive-compulsive believes that failure to neutralize perceived threat will lead to dangerous consequences (e.g., hurting others, losing control, contamination, fire, burglary, and so on).

Beck's model is similar to Richard Lazarus's stress-appraisal model (see Lazarus and Folkman 1984). According to Lazarus, there are two stages in the development of anxiety or stress. The first stage—primary appraisal—involves the evaluation of threat: "Is there an imminent threat to self?" The second stage—secondary appraisal—involves the individual's perception of his ability to handle that threat: "Do I have the resources available to keep the threat from harming me?" If the answer to the second question is no, the individual experiences anxiety or stress. According to Beck's model, the anxious patient believes that threats are all around or within her, and he does not have the resources to handle them. Furthermore, the anxious individual often focuses on her anxiety symptoms (heart pounding, stammering, mind going blank) as factors that further incapacitate her. Thus, the more anxious she becomes, the less able she feels in handling the threat. Example:

> A woman suffering from panic disorder would become anxious at the health club during exercise. As her heart rate increased and

she breathed more rapidly, she thought: "I won't be able to catch my breath" or "I'll die of a heart attack." Because of these frequent false alarms, she began to avoid her exercise classes.

Cognitive Distortions in Anxiety

As indicated earlier, the anxious patient has characteristic cognitive distortions. These typical cognitive distortions may be divided into three groups: automatic thoughts, maladaptive assumptions, and schemas.

Automatic Thoughts

Catastrophizing: Something terrible is going to happen. I am going to die.
Mislabeling: My heart pounding means I am having a heart attack.
Dichotomous thinking: I am always anxious.
Overgeneralizing: I can't handle my anxiety. I can't handle anything.

Maladaptive Assumptions (or Rules)

I must get rid of all anxiety—immediately and forever.
Anxiety and arousal are dangerous.
If people knew that I was anxious, they would reject me.
Anxiety is a sign of weakness. I should never be weak.
I shouldn't be anxious.
I have to watch out for my anxiety so it doesn't catch me by surprise.

Schemas

Biological threat: Anxiety means I'm dying.
Humiliation: People will laugh at me.
Control: I am either in complete control or I have no control.
Autonomy: Anxiety means I have no mobility. I have to get out of here.
Abandonment: I will be abandoned. I can't survive on my own.

A man with panic disorder and social phobia would become anxious over the thought that he might be trapped in a van with co-workers. His automatic thought was: "I'll have an anxiety attack and I won't make any sense when I start talking." His maladaptive assumption was: "If I am anxious, people will be able to see it and they will think I'm inferior." His underlying self-schema and schemas about others were: "I'm basically inferior and weak" and "People are rejecting and humiliating." His developmental history revealed a father who demanded that he be more competent than anyone else and, when he could not achieve these standards, his father would humiliate and hit him.

Coping Strategies

As the cognitive model has developed over the last ten years there has been an increasing emphasis on modifying the maladaptive assumptions and personal schemas associated with anxiety. For example, anxious individuals may develop life-long patterns of compensating for their anxiety or avoiding situations that elicit it. The avoidant personality copes with her anxiety about rejection by requiring guarantees of acceptance before she will enter a relationship. The dependent personality develops excellent abilities in pleasing others in order to avoid abandonment.

Each of the anxiety disorders is characterized by attempts to cope with perceived threat. The social phobic scans his environment for any signs of rejection, engaging in mind-reading, negative prediction, and selective filtering of negatives while discounting positives. The social phobic believes that public humiliation may be avoided by noticing these signs of rejection and escaping from the situation as soon as possible. Similarly, the obsessive-compulsive believes that his focus on the dangers of contamination will prevent him from making a mistake that would lead to unrelenting regret and self-criticism. The cognitive therapist, using the techniques outlined in subsequent chapters, assists the patient in identifying these underlying maladaptive strategies and helps him acquire cognitive and behavioral skills to overcome these problems.

ANGER AND MARITAL DISCORD

Anger

The cognitive model of anger overlaps considerably with Beck's model (forthcoming) of anxiety. Here he traces the origins of the anger mode to ethological considerations. In our discussion of anxiety, the response to anxiety is seen as the result of the evolution of defensive patterns. With anger, the individual is preadapted to respond to threats to safety or resources with an aggressive response. Similar to Lorenz (1966), Eibl-Eibesfeldt (1975), and Wilson (1975), one can view anger and aggression as providing an adaptive response that assures defense of territory, spacing of individuals throughout the surrounding areas, defense of nesting sites, protection against sexual competition, and immediate defense against attack. In addition, aggression may assist members of the group in pursuing greater advantage in the dominance hierarchy with its consequent opportunities for material and sexual resources (see Buss [1994] for a discussion of the evolution of sexual competitiveness and choice). Wilson's theory of sociobiology stresses the importance of group selection (not just individual selection) in the evolution of shared defensive or aggressive behavior. Specifically, the individual may be willing to sacrifice personal advantage in order to defend the group, precisely because he is of the same genetic structure (conferring some advantage on him), and because this altruistic aggression or shared aggression allows him to benefit from the protection of the group.

Many of the physiological responses in aggression may be understood from the perspective of the ethological approach. Increased heart rate, visual narrowing of the field, muscle tension, increased muscular ability and strength in the immediate situation, clenching of the fists and jaws, baring the teeth, all confer a threat to others in the immediate environment and provide the individual with the readiness to respond swiftly with aggression. (One should also note that there are important differences in the hunting or predator response, with its greater stealth and planning, and the aggressive-angry response that is a preadapted response to threat. It is the anger-aggression response that we refer to here.)

The anger response is a result of the individual's appraisal that someone has provoked him by insult, threatened injury, or violated important rules. Thus, the individual becomes angry because he believes that another has intentionally insulted him. The individual believes that this insult will lower his own position socially (or lower his self-esteem—a private injury). We also become angry and defensive when we believe that others wish to cause us injury (for example, threats to our material well-being, our family, or our access to resources). Anger and aggression also result when we perceive others as violating rules that we believe are important to uphold, even when the violation of the rule may not have immediate relevance to our own interests. (See James Wilson's [1993] discussion in *The Moral Sense* of why all societies may have evolved a shared moral code emphasizing obligation, delay of gratification, and fairness.)

There are typical automatic thought distortions that surface when individuals become angry and aggressive. Examples of these are:

Labeling: He's a rotten person. He can't be trusted.
Personalizing: Why did he do that to me?
Blaming: It's all her fault. She's the one who ruined the relationship.
Catastrophizing: I can't stand it when she does that!
All-or-nothing thinking: She's always screwing up. We're always arguing.
Fortune-telling: This will go on forever. There's no end to it.
Mind-reading: He's really trying to get me angry.

Of course, as with any automatic thought, there is a chance that the thought is true. However, research shows consistent patterns of excessive physiological arousal among people who are angry in response to their greater predisposition to perceive provocation. The angry individual is more likely to interpret neutral events as intentionally directed against him, thus justifying his angry response (Dodge and Coie 1987).

Angry or retaliatory responses are also affected by the individual's ability to use information that mitigates or lessens anger. For example, we have found that individuals are more likely to calm their anger if they believe that the transgressor was himself provoked, acting under duress, lacked foresight that his behavior would be injurious, or was suffering from emotional problems (Leahy 1981, 1983). Very likely, the individual's anger is lessened when he is less likely to infer intentionality of the transgression, personalize the behavior, or perceive the individual as likely to continue with the aggression again. Not surprisingly, transgressors who are viewed as sincerely sorry that they committed the act are more likely to be forgiven (Leahy 1979, 1983).

Anger escalates with the proliferation of rules that the individual sees as violated. As Horney notes, the individual suffers from the "tyranny of the shoulds." The angry individual has two levels of shoulds. First, "You shouldn't do x, y or z" and second, "You should be punished (for your violation of the should)." Moreover, the angry individual has a set of maladaptive assumptions and contingency statements: "If you violate the rule, you are a bad person" and "If you disagree with me, you are against me." These assumption and shoulds become the rules that lead to escalation of anger and retaliation.

Anger is often related to the individual's perception that the other person may threaten a schematic issue. For example, some people become angry if they believe their special status is threatened, they are being rejected or abandoned, or they are being controlled. The therapist can assist the patient in understanding what the meaning of the alleged provocation might be. "Was he really trying to provoke you or was it unintentional? Can there be another explanation for his behavior?"

According to the cognitive model, anger is focused on externalizing blame. Consequently, angry individuals have an egoistic bias—that is, they seldom view themselves as the cause of the other person's "transgression." One can argue that anger or externalization is viewed by some as an attempt to maintain self-esteem in the blame game. Because the focus is external, rather than interactional, the angry individual retaliates and then condemns the other person's response to the retaliation. The cognitive therapist may assist the patient in understanding interactional patterns, such as coercion cycles, in which both individuals are reinforcing the other's negative behavior and eliciting retaliatory responses (Patterson 1982, Tedeschi and Felson 1994). Training in role-taking and empathy helps the angry individual understand how others might feel when they are the target of retaliation.

Models of anger control in cognitive therapy differ from catharsis models that stress the expression rather than the control of anger. Unlike dynamic or expressive models that propose that the individual needs to overtly express his anger lest it be turned inward, the cognitive approach argues that the activation of anger facilitates or disinhibits further expression of anger. Thus, once the individual begins expressing his anger, it activates more angry feelings, memories, and perceptions, further engendering more anger. Furthermore, the expression of anger often leads to rejecting or hostile responses from others. These hostile responses further exacerbate the individual's anger. Few people become less angry by becoming more angry.

The cognitive treatment of anger is based on Meichenbaum's (1974) stress inoculation model (Novaco 1978). Specifically, the therapist assists the individual in identifying the physiological signs of anger (clenched jaws, rapid heart beat), the situations most likely to elicit anger (discriminative stimuli), and the behavioral signs of aggression in the self (loud voice, hostile labeling comments). The patient is asked to consider the costs and benefits of becoming more aggressive (eliciting aggression in others, getting fired or divorced). The therapist assists the patient in identifying alternatives to aggression, for example: responsible assertion, time out, withdrawal, problem solving, and questioning one's own negative thinking. The patient and therapist engage in role-playing exercises that assist the patient in rehearsing the appropriate coping strategies in dealing with situations that mimic provocation. In the chapter on marital therapy, I will describe how the therapist can assist the couple in reducing hostile interactions by the use of these procedures.

Marital Discord

Similar to marriage itself, the cognitive-behavioral model of relationships is complex and multifaceted. This will be seen more clearly in Chapter 9, but the reader may also wish to consult the excellent text by Baucom and Epstein (1990), *Cognitive-Behavioral Marital Therapy.* Here I use the term *marital*, but indeed we are describing almost any relationship discord.

Behavioral models of marriage are based on the importance of rewards and punishments in the relationship. On first thought, one might suppose that the greater the reward, the better the relationship. However, Gottman (1995) has found that it is the ratio of rewards to punishments, not the sheer amount, that counts. Marriages that exceed ratios of five rewards to one punishment (or averse consequence) are experienced as relatively satisfying. Gottman goes further and describes the various styles of marital partners. For example, some partners are ventilators and like to express strong feelings; others are validators and like to have their feelings recognized and understood. Some partners prefer rational or companionate relationships. Depending on the style, there will be a need for more or fewer rewards. For example, a relationship of ventilation (with many opportunities for negative experiences) can be experienced as satisfactory if there is a high number and frequency of rewards to offset the negatives.

As may seem obvious, behavioral approaches to marriage attempt to increase rewards and decrease negatives. The assumption for some therapists is that individuals calculate a social-exchange formula: "Given the ratio of costs and benefits in this relationship, can I get a better trade-off somewhere else? Would being alone give me a better deal or would another partner?" (Jacobson and Margolin 1980).

From the cognitive model, one cannot know beforehand

what is rewarding and what is aversive to individuals. Further-more, the motivation to give positives to your partner may depend on a number of cognitive factors: "Do you label your partner in negative ways? Do you personalize your partner's every behavior? Do you catastrophize negatives?" Fincham (1985) and Baucom (1987) have studied the dysfunctional attributional or explanatory styles of distressed partners, finding they are more likely to attribute negative intentions to their partner, globalize, personalize, and infer that their partner has negative personality traits that are difficult, if not impossible, to change.

In addition to dysfunctional attributional styles, distressed partners are more likely to have perfectionist standards, expectations of entitlement, reciprocity standards that are negative ("an eye for an eye"), and excessive need for approval and compliance from their partners. Recently, cognitive therapists have examined the importance of personal schemas in relationships (Datillio and Padesky 1990). For example, if the distressed partner believes that she is not recognized or understood by people, she will view simple differences in styles of communication as invalidation and rejection. Another example of a personal schema is the belief that the healthy independence of the spouse is an indication of abandonment. These schemas of invalidation and abandonment then contribute to maladaptive rules in the relationship. For example, the husband who focuses on the issue of invalidation will question his wife's motives, while the wife who focuses on abandonment will seek reassurance that her husband is not leaving her.

Cognitive-behavioral models of marital conflict also focus on the importance of effective communication. Stuart's (1980) model of communication proposes that empathy and the feeling that one is understood and respected are key to the relationship. One could ask, "Why be involved if you are not going to feel that your partner cares about what you think and feel?" Consequently, behavioral interventions focus on training couples in effective speaking skills (learning to talk about their own feelings and not the other's personality traits) and effective skills in listening (rephrasing what your partner says, empathizing, and inquiring).

Finally, behavioral models of marriage view relationship conflict as arising from a failure in problem-solving. Distressed partners may fail to identify their conflicts as problems to solve, or they may identify too many problems, or they may present unsolvable problems ("You need to change your entire personality!"). The inability to apply problem-solving or negotiation skills results in a proliferation of unresolved problems for couples, further adding to their sense of hopelessness and depression. Interventions focus on the acquisition of problem-solving skills.

4

BASIC PRINCIPLES

In describing basic principles, one can only imagine the difficulty in attempting to reduce a rapidly growing field to a few generally shared ideas. In fact, the idea of cognitive-behavioral therapy would have seemed like a contradiction to a "pure" radical behaviorist like B. F. Skinner in the 1970s. Behaviorism was not only a psychological approach but a philosophical position that rejected any discussion of thoughts and feelings as meaningless, unverifiable, and unscientific.

The field has changed greatly in the last twenty years. Few practicing therapists still adhere to a radical behavioral model in which thinking and feeling are viewed as noise in the "black box." Behavior therapists, such as Lewinsohn and Jacobson, whose earlier operant models would have been consistent with Skinner's ideas, now incorporate significant cognitive interventions and concepts in their treatment recommendations. Similarly, Beck and Ellis utilize a variety of behavioral interventions in their cognitive or rational approaches. Indeed, the Association for the Advancement of Behavior Therapy (AABT) may soon be called the Association for the Advancement of Cognitive-Behavioral Therapy.

As we indicated, cognitive therapy is not based on any single theoretical model or set of techniques. Given the rapid growth of cognitive therapy, it is important to identify which principles and practices are commonly endorsed in cognitive therapy. In this chapter we review twenty basic principles and practices generally reflected in cognitive therapy practice.

1. Focus on Behavior and Cognition

Unlike psychodynamic or client-centered approaches that focus on unconscious thoughts or feelings and emphasize catharsis during therapy, cognitive therapy emphasizes current behavior and conscious thought. Assessment begins with an evaluation of the behavioral deficits and excesses of the patient and the pattern of conscious thought associated with depression, anxiety, anger, or relationship conflict. The goal is to modify both behavior and cognition rather than to provide an opportunity for the patient simply to ventilate his or her feelings. The assumption is that changes in behavior and cognition will produce changes in feelings.

2. Present-Time Orientation

Cognitive therapy is less interested in the early history of the patient than in his or her current functioning. Although the therapist will take a life-history, the emphasis is more on how current thinking, behavior, rewards, and punishments maintain a dysfunctional pattern. In recent years, some cognitive therapists have utilized developmental analysis or focused on early maladaptive schemas, but the purpose of this focus is only to challenge the current thinking and modify the current behavior of the patient. The emphasis is less on "Why am I this way?" and more on "What do I have to do to change?"

3. Short-Term Therapy

Cognitive therapy is relatively short-term in duration. Many studies of treatment efficacy utilize treatment packages for twenty or fewer sessions. The emphasis in short-term therapy is to eliminate symptoms and help the patient acquire self-help skills, rather than attempt to change his personality or provide him with a transference relationship. Not only is therapy short-term, but patients may complete work on one problem (e.g., panic disorder) and return at a later time to work on another focused problem (e.g., marital conflict).

4. Emphasis on Measurement

From the first intake evaluation to the final session, cognitive therapy will attempt to measure change by evaluating specific symptoms for frequency, duration, intensity, and severity. Rather than forming a vague impression ("The patient is depressed"), this therapy assesses the specific level and nature of the depression ("This patient has a score of 25 on the Beck Depression Inventory with elevations in hopelessness, self-criticism, and loss of interest in other people").

5. Accountability

Utilizing the measurements obtained during the initial assessments and throughout therapy, cognitive therapy may be evaluated by both therapist and patient for its accountability. During the first few sessions the patient and therapist will agree on a therapeutic contract to work on specific problems or symptoms. Progress (or lack of progress) in working on these problems will be assessed, using measurements obtained periodically. Accountability is further enhanced by asking patients for feedback about sessions. Some therapists formalize this process by having patients complete therapy evaluation forms after sessions.

6. Collaboration

The relationship between patient and therapist is collaborative for it is assumed that both are trying to work toward the same goals. Moreover, patients will be asked to provide their suggestions for goals to work on, how therapy sessions can be modified, and what homework the patient might assign himself.

7. Didactic

Cognitive therapy views the patient as partly in a learning role, whether it involves learning more about her problems, acquiring self-help or social skills, or learning how to modify her thinking and behavior. Many therapists use bibliotherapy; that is, they recommend books, pamphlets, or other materials for patients to read. The therapist often serves as a model of appropriate behavior and thinking. For example, the therapist might demonstrate to the patient how a less anxious or depressed individual might think or behave. Part of the didactic component is that the patient will practice or rehearse in session the skills that will be generalized in homework assignments. The assumption is that the more the patient knows, the better he will be able to cope with his problem.

8. Foster Independence

The ideal for the patient in cognitive therapy is to achieve independent functioning—to put the therapist out of business. Independence is enhanced by emphasizing learning, behavior rehearsal, self-help homework assignments, increasing assertive behavior, troubleshooting problems that might occur outside of therapy or when therapy is discontinued, and helping the patient enhance his or her social network. By encouraging patients to provide the therapist with feedback, the therapist reinforces the patient's independent thinking and assertiveness.

9. Consumer Model

Patients are individuals with life problems who are also consumers. Consequently, cognitive therapy views them as informed consumers who are apprised of the costs and benefits of treatment, the plan of therapy, and the viable alternatives. The informed consumer position may be reinforced by clearly indicating to the patient exactly what is expected of him or her. For example, in treating the obsessive-compulsive patient, the therapist may indicate that exposure to feared stimuli will probably increase anxiety before reducing it. The patient's freedom to choose is enhanced by the therapist's urging the patient to weigh the costs and benefits of his or her recommendations.

10. Targeted Symptoms

Cognitive therapy focuses on specific symptoms for change. Behavior therapists refer to these as targets, indicating that the purpose of therapy is to increase or decrease specific behaviors, thoughts, feelings, or interactions. The emphasis on targets, rather than vague improvement, is so that the patient can more easily evaluate and modify specific targeted symptoms and thereby see progress more clearly.

11. Rejection of Symptom Substitution

Cognitive therapy rejects the idea of symptom substitution—the concept that a symptom is the "economic" solution to an underlying neurotic process. Rather, the emphasis is on symptom elimination or reduction, with the assumption that a reduction in symptoms in one area (e.g., reduction of panic) will lead to improvement in other areas (e.g., decrease in depression).

12. Emphasis on Continual Change

The goal of each session is to help the patient to change—indeed, to rehearse changing in the session. For example, the patient will be asked to practice new behaviors and cognitions in the session and to generalize these outside the session as part of homework. Change is viewed as a cumulative process with patients practicing new behaviors outside of sessions and gaining greater skills and rewards from this change.

13. Rejection of "Readiness For Change"

Cognitive therapy generally rejects the idea that the patient has to be "ready" for change. Rather, the emphasis is on acting *against* your beliefs, that is, acting *as if* you were ready for change. The assumption is that the patient must be encouraged to practice new behaviors and cognitions *even if they do not yet feel comfortable with them*. In this sense, the patient is continuously challenged to change in spite of the fact that he may not feel ready to change.

14. Challenging the Patient's Position

Whether we view this as evaluating, testing, or challenging the patient's behavior and beliefs, cognitive therapy actively confronts the patient with the idea that there are alternatives to her habitual patterns. In pursuit of this self-questioning model, the patient is asked to challenge her own thinking.

15. Problem-Solving Focus

Each session is viewed as an opportunity to make progress in solving problems rather than simply ventilating, complaining, or asking for emotional support. The therapist may even raise this issue by asking the patient at the beginning of the session, "What problem do you want me to help you solve today?" At the end of the session, the therapist may ask if the patient believes he has made progress in how to solve that problem. Problem solving is enhanced by asking the patient for specific goals, examination of alternatives, development of plans, and carrying out of experiments.

16. Use of Treatment Plans

Therapy may follow specific treatment plans for various problems. For panic disorder the therapist and patient may collaborate on developing plans for exposure to feared stimuli, recognizing distorted thinking related to panic symptoms, relaxation training, and reducing stress. Cognitive therapy does not just shoot from the hip, but rather structures therapy according to a sequence of interventions and evaluations.

17. Continuity across Sessions

Using treatment plans assists the therapist in providing a sense of continuity across sessions. In each session the therapist will review the previous week's homework assignments, a current problem, and plans for the following week. Periodic evaluation of progress on specific problems helps patient and therapist determine whether therapy is addressing the patient's concerns.

18. Demystifying Therapy

As the foregoing illustrates, the plan and in-session process takes the mystery out of therapy for the patient. Using biblio-therapy, treatment plans, modeling, behavioral rehearsal, homework, and accountability, the patient is drawn into a respectful collaborative relationship with the therapist. Questions about interventions or resistances that the patient has to assignments are directly addressed, thereby providing him with information.

19. Requesting Patient Feedback

The process of therapy and the therapist's own behavior are constantly open to modification. The therapist asks the patient to tell her of any change in emotion (positive or negative) so that she and the patient can better understand what works and what does not work. The assumption is that no one therapy works for everyone so the patient's input is invaluable. Problems in homework compliance often may be avoided by asking the patient to demonstrate in session how he will carry out the homework, what is unclear, or what reasons he might have for not doing the homework.

20. Empirically Based Treatments

Cognitive therapy has been widely tested with a variety of psychological disorders including depression, anxiety, panic, obsessive-compulsive disorder, marital conflict, substance abuse, conduct disorders of childhood, and attention-deficit disorder with hyperactivity. The therapist can feel comfortable knowing that hundreds of studies demonstrate the efficacy and lasting effectiveness of many of these techniques. The productive interaction of researchers and practitioners of cognitive therapy assures that the therapist will have access to methods and techniques based on proven treatment approaches.

These twenty principles indicate how cognitive therapy differs from psychodynamic or client-centered supportive therapies. Certainly, we recognize that psychodynamic therapists will, on occasion, focus on the present time or on the need for the patient to change, but these twenty principles reflect a qualitatively different orientation toward the conduct of therapy.

Some critics of this therapy may argue that feelings are ignored or that the therapy is too technique-oriented or that the therapist appears to be more a technician and less an empathic human being. In reality, however, the goal of therapy is to change feelings, not to ignore them. Some patients may complain that they expected to have more opportunity to ventilate their feelings. We have found it useful to negotiate this as part of the agenda-setting in sessions: for example, therapist and patient agree to spend the first ten minutes with the patient expressing her feelings and the therapist listening empathically. However, the remainder of the session is focused on modifying the patient's bulimia.

Some beginning therapists may focus more on techniques and lose sight of the individuality of the patient. Moreover, the focus on technique may obscure their ability to empathize with the patient. However, research by DeRubeis and Feeley (1990) indicates that therapists who comply with the cognitive therapy model and produce changes in depression are viewed as more empathic than therapists not following the techniques. A common-sense interpretation of this is that patients appreciate both a structured approach and change in their depression.

Another criticism of cognitive therapy is that it does not deal with "deeper issues." What these critics mean by "deeper issues" is often unclear. Our response to this is fourfold. First, patients pursue therapy seeking symptom relief, not understanding per se. Relief of symptoms is a reasonable and perhaps primary ethical goal of treatment. Second, many patients show substantial improvement in a brief treatment format and, when homework compliance is maintained, improvement can still be seen two years later. Consequently, one might argue that whatever deeper issues are present, there is no evidence of a need for longer-term treatment for a majority of patients. Third, we would agree with these critics regarding a minority of patients, especially those whose dysthymia or personality disorders are a major source of recurrent problems or resistance to treatment. Recent advances in cognitive therapy (Beck and Freeman 1990, Leahy 1985, 1992, 1995, Young 1990) attempt to address how it can be modified to help patients with personality disorders. Fourth, we believe that therapists who can help patients rapidly overcome long-standing problems such as panic disorder or obsessive-compulsive disorder will have considerable credibility with patients seeking help with other problems, such as personality disorder. There is no better intervention than an effective intervention.

II

ASSESSMENT AND INTERVENTIONS

5

BEHAVIORAL INTERVENTIONS

Although I recognize that cognitive-behavioral therapy is now a "hyphenated" therapy (although some therapists prefer either "cognitive" or "behavioral") there are a variety of techniques more clearly associated with traditional behavior therapy. Behavior therapy traces its historical roots to the pioneering work of John Watson on acquired fears, and to the significant contributions of B. F. Skinner, John Dollard, and Neal Miller. Behavior therapists, however, had attempted to move beyond the discussions of general principles of behavior and to develop a set of interventions ostensibly based on learning principles.

Cognitive-behavioral therapy refers to a range of therapeutic approaches and interventions that, to various degrees, draw upon traditional behavioral techniques. In this chapter we review the basic concepts, techniques, and interventions that comprise more traditional behavioral approaches. However, as will be clear in subsequent discussions, behavioral techniques are *always* included in cognitive therapy.

BEHAVIORAL ASSESSMENT

Adult disorders may be evaluated using behavioral assessments. Self-monitoring of targeted behaviors is a simple, informative, and often powerful assessment and intervention. For example, patients complaining about anxiety or physical pain may be asked to record the degree of their anxiety or pain for every hour of the week. One patient, presenting with headaches estimated at ninety hours per week, showed a dramatic reduction in frequency and intensity of headaches simply by self-monitoring. He discovered that his headaches were most severe when he was arguing with his father or driving in traffic.

Part of behavioral assessment is to identify what will be observed and recorded. We encourage patients to keep daily records of targeted behaviors, clearly defined with the patient's assistance. For example, in assessing and treating shyness in a female patient, the therapist requested that the patient record all examples of positive social behavior directed by other people toward her. Positive social behavior was defined as smiling, looking at, approaching, talking to, touching, complimenting, and asking questions of the patient. The rationale for this assignment was that the patient was not listening for positives in others. Subsequent to this assignment, the patient was asked to keep track of all her positive social behaviors directed toward others. These assessments proved to be powerful interventions in modifying her social shyness.

Another aspect of behavioral assessment is to identify situational antecedents and consequences of behaviors (in self and others). Since the behavioral model is based on the view that certain stimuli elicit behavior and other stimuli reinforce behavior, it is important to examine the antecedents and consequences that maintain behavior. For example, a husband may complain about his wife's lack of attention. The therapist might ask him to keep track of all examples of her attention (with targeted behaviors defined) and exactly what he does when she does attend to him. The question addressed here is whether the husband attends to and rewards the wife.

Behavioral assessments also include general classes of behaviors of specific interest to the clinician in evaluating the patient. For example, the therapist may be interested in knowing what situations the patient avoids, how much the patient drinks (and where and with whom he drinks), which behaviors the patient engages in that could be construed as assertive, and which sexual behaviors partners pursue (and how often and with what degree of satisfaction). The clinician may develop his or her own behavioral measures or use self-report forms for specific classes of behaviors. In this chapter, we will examine how the cognitive-behavioral therapist uses behavioral assessment and interventions.

BEHAVIORAL SELECTION

Target Behaviors. A hallmark of a strictly behavioral approach is the focus on observable, measurable, discrete behaviors. For example, in the treatment of childhood enuresis, the behavior therapist will focus on changing the target behavior—bedwetting—and will have the client (usually the parent) measure the occurrences, even the size of the stain left. Target behaviors are important in cognitive-behavioral therapy, although seldom are these behaviors measured on such a molecular level. Examples of target behaviors might be specific social interactions, exercise, number of times the patient rewards his or her spouse, exposure to threatening situations, or shared activities with the spouse. One might argue, in fact, that target behaviors are such an important part of cognitive-behavioral therapy that the effectiveness of the therapy can be assessed by changes in the patient's behavior.

In any behavioral intervention the first step is to select the behaviors that are to be modified. For example, in training social skills, the therapist cannot offer the vague and general statement: "We must improve your social skills"; rather, she will attempt to identify specific behaviors that are to be increased or decreased in frequency, intensity, or quality. Similar to those of the experimental psychologist, these targeted behaviors are operationally defined. The operational definition refers to concrete, specific behavioral examples. For example, the general category of positive social approach can be operationally defined by the following specific behaviors: smiling, initiating conversations, asking questions, complimenting others, and touching.

Deficits and Excesses. In developing interventions, the therapist needs to determine which behaviors are deficits (not occurring frequently or effectively enough) and which behaviors are excesses (occurring too frequently or intensely). Examples of low-frequency deficits of the following behavioral categories are: personal hygiene, assertiveness, positive recreational behaviors, social contacts, self-rewards, sleep, and productive work-related behaviors. The goal in therapy is to increase the frequency of these behavioral deficits.

Examples of behavioral excesses include those related to substance abuse, consumption of high-calorie foods, complaining, criticizing, self-mutilation, and absence from work or school. These behaviors are targets to be decreased.

Often the functional analysis of behavior will indicate that behavioral deficits receive few rewards and behavioral excesses receive frequent rewards. For example, the low frequency of a wife's affectionate behavior (a behavioral deficit) is related to the low probability of her affectionate behavior being rewarded (when the wife is affectionate the husband ignores her). Similarly, the high frequency of a child's yelling is related to the high probability that when he yells, he'll get attention, but when he speaks in a normal tone he is ignored.

In contrast to the psychodynamic model that views symptoms as an economic compromise or solution to the patient's anxiety, the behavioral approach views symptoms as the central problem. These symptoms are behaviors, thoughts, and emotions. Theoretically, once they are changed, the problem is alleviated. Rather than expect symptom substitution, the cognitive-behavioral therapist expects to see improvement in one area generalize to improvement in another area. For example, improvement in panic and agoraphobia leads to an improvement in the marital relationship

Establishing Baseline. Behavior therapists approach interventions with an experimental model by which specific changes are continuously evaluated. For example, in training the patient in social skills the therapist will establish the pre-intervention baseline—the level of specific target behaviors prior to applying interventions. Baselines should refer to the specific frequency, duration, or consequence of the targeted behavior. For example, during the past week how frequently did the patient initiate conversations? How long were these conversations maintained? Did these conversations result in specific positive consequences? By establishing the baseline of targeted behaviors, patient and therapist can evaluate how effective interventions are.

Other examples of baseline measures are the frequency and duration of headaches, intensity of headaches, amount of medication taken, number of times the patient pulls her hair, number of hours of exercise, number of cigarettes smoked, and number of times the patient asserts herself with others.

These baseline measures are then repeated daily hopefully, and patient and therapist evaluate the change since baseline. Simply taking baseline measures and monitoring targeted symptoms are often sufficient to modify the symptom. This may be due to the patient becoming more mindful or conscious of her behavior, thereby directing greater self-control toward the targeted behavior.

Multiple baselines refer to the use of more than one measure or behavior at baseline. For example, in training social skills we would want a sampling of numerous behaviors in a variety of situations. If we limited our assessment to a single behavior (e.g., asking others out for dates), we might not find any progress for months. On the other hand, if we assessed ten different positive social behaviors, we might find that several of these behaviors have increased in frequency. Since depressed patients have a negative filter and are likely to focus on the one thing that has not changed, it is useful for the therapist to use multiple baselines.

EVALUATION OF BEHAVIOR AND FUNCTIONAL ANALYSIS

Continuous Evaluation. Behavior therapists evaluate change from the beginning to the end of therapy. Ideally, evaluations are made weekly, although many therapists may feel satisfied with intermittent or periodic evaluations. The advantage of continuous evaluation is that both patient and therapist can note even the smallest change in a behavior or mood. As evaluations proceed, the targets may change. For example, in a social-skills treatment package, the patient may initially focus on smiling and making eye contact with others, but shift to more demanding targets such as starting conversations or asking people out. Detailed records of targeted behaviors that have changed offer the patient considerable pleasure in seeing progress unfold.

Discriminative Stimulus. The individual does not respond equally to all stimuli. For example, the gourmet might respond with greater salivation to the sight of Italian food than to Swedish food. The ability to discriminate between these two cuisines is linked to their different reinforcing potentials. The question in a behavioral analysis is, "Which stimuli lead to reinforcements or punishments for the individual?" Can the individual discriminate between situations so linked to different outcomes? Stimuli can become more easily discriminated by changing their salient features (size, intensity, relevance), verbal labeling, and by clearly and consistently associating differential consequences.

Differential Reinforcement of Other Behavior (DRO). DRO refers to the fact that the individual is engaged in one behavior at a time. If we reinforce Behavior 1, then during that period Behavior 2 will less likely occur. Consider two behaviors— playing quietly with toys (Behavior 1) and throwing toys (Behavior 2). If we reinforce playing quietly with toys (Behavior 1), and ignore throwing toys (Behavior 2), then we should expect that Behavior 1 will increase as Behavior 2 decreases.

DRO is the principle behind positive tracking in marital or child-behavior therapy. For example, many distressed spouses focus only on the negative behavior of their partner, seldom either noticing or reinforcing the positive behavior. The attention directed toward the negative may, in fact, be a reinforcement for the "misbehaving" spouse, since he at least gets the interest or arouses the anger of his partner. By having the wife differentially focus and reward only positives, the opportunity to attend to and reinforce negatives is decreased. Thus, differential reinforcement for other behavior leads to an increase in the positive and a decrease in the negative. An advantage of DRO is that punitive responses are decreased, since the patient is encouraged to focus on positives and consequently generally becomes more optimistic.

Functional Analysis.   Behaviorists refer to the A–B–C paradigm—that is, Antecedents, Behavior, Consequences. This is known as the *functional analysis of behavior* because the therapist is interested in what elicits the behavior and what reinforces (or punishes) the behavior. Table 5–1 illustrates some examples of this concept.

As inspection of Table 5–1 indicates, both positive and negative behavior can be reinforced or punished. For example, initiating conversation (a positive social behavior) can be reinforced and the wife's request to the husband can be punished.

Functional analysis is important because it tells us what maintains the individual's behavior. In marital therapy the emphasis will be on increasing positive consequences of positive behavior. Functional analysis for couples presenting with marital discord generally reveals that positive behavior is often ignored or even punished; consequently positive behavior decreases in frequency. Moreover, functional analysis indicates that negative behavior (e.g., the demanding behavior of the oppositional child) is often rewarded; the child screams for candy and gets candy.

The cognitive-behavioral therapist may extend functional

Table 5–1. Functional Analysis of Behavior

Antecedents	Behavior	Consequences
In bakery	Buy and eat donut	Feel satiated Self-criticism
See man at party	Initiate conversation	He compliments me
Wife makes request	I argue and refuse	Wife withdraws
Child yells for candy	I give him candy	Child stops yelling

analysis to determine the internal consequences of a behavior. For example, when the depressed person engages in positive behavior, does he or she self-reward? Rehm's (1977) self-control model proposes that depression often results from the failure to reward the self for positive behavior. In fact many depressed people will even punish themselves for positive behavior: "Yeah, I initiated a conversation, but I sounded like an idiot."

Self-Monitoring: When, Where, How Much.   The simplest, least intrusive intervention involves self-monitoring. The patient must have a clear behavior, thought, or emotion that will be monitored. For example, the patient can keep track of the number of times during the week he or she engages in self-criticism, experiences variations in anxiety, or engages in specific behaviors. Self-monitoring yields a number of desirable effects or information: the patient and therapist obtain information about (1) how time is used, (2) variations of mood associated with emotions and thoughts, (3) diurnal variations of mood. In addition, self-monitoring (4) increases the patient's awareness of what he or she is doing, and (5) this increased self-awareness may enhance self-control by increasing the mindfulness for the patient (Langer 1989). Self-monitoring should be documented so the patient need not rely on memory to recollect facts.

The patient is asked to record specific targeted behaviors, noting when and where and how much of the behavior occurs. For example, in training assertiveness the therapist will be interested in when and where (or with whom) the patient does or does not assert. The patient may be assertive with her employees but not with her husband. This information is useful because it may indicate that the patient has the skills to assert but defines situations in terms of their appropriateness for assertion.

CONDITIONING PARADIGMS

Behavioral interventions are based on models of learning, concepts of reinforcement, punishment, extinction, schedules of reinforcement, and imitation. All operant conditioning paradigms are based on the law of effect, which states that the frequency (or intensity) of a behavior is a function of the consequence (effects) that the behavior produces. Specifically, behavior that is reinforced increases in frequency and behavior that is punished decreases in frequency. Thus, if the husband only pays attention to his wife when she raises her voice, then she will be more likely to raise her voice in the future. And, if the husband criticizes his wife's sexual overtures, she will be less likely to approach him in the future.

There are two kinds of reinforcement, positive and negative. In both cases, reinforcement always increases the frequency of a behavior. *Positive reinforcement* refers to any condition in which the consequence increases the likelihood of a behavior in the future: for example, if the child requests candy, the mother gives the child candy. This increases requests for candy in the future.

Negative reinforcement refers to situations where the consequence terminates an aversive stimulus: for example, if the mother hits the child for yelling (an aversive stimulus)—and the child stops yelling—the mother's hitting is negatively reinforced because it terminates the child's yelling. Consequently, we would expect that this reinforcement will increase the possibility of her hitting the child in the future.

Punishment refers to situations where the consequence decreases a behavior. For example, if you park your car in front of a fire hydrant and your car is towed (punishment), you will be less likely to park your car in front of hydrants in the future.

Avoidance conditioning refers to a situation in which the individual avoids contact with a feared stimulus, thereby avoiding an increase in anxiety. For example, the individual who fears elevators refuses to get onto the elevator. This avoidance behavior is reinforced because it decreases the likelihood of an increase in anxiety. Similarly, the social phobic feels anxious when speaking in public. Consequently, he avoids any work that might put him in the position of speaking in public and so his anxiety does not increase. Interestingly, patients who use avoidance conditioning as a coping style may often present with very little symptomatic anxiety, for they are successfully avoiding situations that make them anxious. One must then ask, "Are there any situations that you avoid? How anxious would you be if you were placed in those situations?"

Escape conditioning is a form of negative reinforcement. It refers to the situation where leaving the field of action by removing oneself from an unpleasant situation results in a decrease in anxiety or fear. For example, if the elevator-phobic gets on the elevator and then leaves (escapes), the escape from the elevator is positively reinforced by the decrease in fear that is a consequence of leaving. Escape conditioning is a key element in agoraphobia, since the patient will attempt to escape from any situation that raises his anxiety. For example, an agoraphobic patient would become anxious at business meetings, fearing that he would get so upset that he might vomit. Although he had never vomited in public, he would get up and leave the meeting as soon as he became anxious. This escape from the meeting was reinforced by a reduction of anxiety; it was positively reinforced since leaving meetings increased in frequency and would occur sooner. (Remember, positive reinforcements always increase the behavior they reinforce.)

Extinction refers to the situation in which a behavior previously reinforced or punished no longer leads to that consequence (i.e., the behavior is ignored). Repeated extinction trials or experiences lead to a decrease in the behavior (if it was previously reinforced) or an increase in the behavior (if it was previously punished). For example, the child who whines for candy (and attention) is consistently ignored, and so we would expect the whining would eventually decrease. Unfortunately, extinction can work with desired behaviors as well. For example, when the wife shows an interest in her husbands's work, but he ignores that interest, her interest in his work will diminish. You will recall from our discussion of differential reinforcement (DRO) that we instructed the husband to attend to and reinforce any attention that his wife pays to his work. Such positive tracking counteracts the extinction noted here.

Shaping is the sequencing of reinforcements such that we reinforce increasing approximations to the final desired behavior. Anyone who has a dog understands this principle. Let us assume we wish to train the dog to sit up and dance. We will begin by reinforcing any behavior that involves facing the trainer; then we will require his lifting one front leg, then both front legs, then turning, and so on. At each point in this sequence, we increase the criterion for reinforcement.

Shaping techniques are used throughout cognitive-behavioral therapy. For example, when we construct a hierarchy of feared situations, from least to most frightening, we are attempting to shape the patient's behavior by having her approach the feared situations in gradual steps. Similarly, when we train patients in assertion, we start off with simple, non-threatening behaviors, such as saying hello, and gradually increase to more demanding behaviors—for example, asking for information, requesting a change in another's behavior, and even making somewhat unreasonable demands on others. In sex therapy for women with orgasmic dysfunction, we might start by requesting that they privately explore their genitals, then engage in masturbation privately, then include their partner in the masturbation, and, finally, pursue penetration with their partner.

Observational learning. According to Bandura (1969), individuals learn through exposure to information (e.g., books, films, observing others) even when the individual is not directly reinforced or punished or shaped into the behavior. This is called observational learning (or imitation). Bandura has shown that the consequences to the observed model affect learning. He refers to this process as *vicarious reinforcement (punishment).* For example, if the individual sees a film in which the model (or character) is reinforced for violence, this will increase the degree to which the observer will imitate that violence. Similarly, if the observer sees the model punished for violent behavior, this will decrease the tendency to imitate the violence. Characteristics of the model (such as similarity to the observer, perceived competence of the model, power, control of reinforcements, and other qualities) will affect the degree to which the model is imitated.

Observational learning or modeling in therapy can be seen when the therapist role-plays responsible assertive behavior or rational responses; the patient is asked to identify someone who successfully engages in behavior he would like to engage in, and then the patient is asked to imitate or act as if he is the role-model.

Reciprocal inhibition. According to traditional behavior therapy (Wolpe 1958), certain responses are incompatible with others. For example, anxiety responses are incompatible with relaxation, sexual release, and assertion. Consequently, anxiety may be inhibited or suppressed if the patient engages in relaxation or sexual or assertive responses. Behaviorists utilize reciprocal inhibition when they have the anxious patient engage in deep-muscle relaxation while simultaneously imagining a fearful stimulus.

Other examples of reciprocal inhibition include teaching the patient to act assertively when he is anxious (assertion inhibits anxiety) or having the patient in sex therapy practice relaxation prior to sex therapy homework (relaxation inhibits anxiety as anxiety inhibits sexual performance). The general rule is that one cannot be anxious and relaxed simultaneously.

Exposure therapy. Continued exposure to a feared stimulus results in a decrease in response strength to that stimulus; the feared stimulus becomes less effective in eliciting any response. Exposure therapy is a form of habituation or satiation. The more often the patient is exposed to a stimulus that she fears and from which she cannot escape the less anxiety the stimulus will arouse. (The patient realizes the feared stimulus is not dangerous and also learns that her anxiety reached a peak and then declined.)

In conducting exposure therapy, therapist and patient construct a series of stimuli or situations (or behaviors) from least to most anxiety-provoking. This stimulus (response) hierarchy then serves as the set of situations or responses for practicing exposure. The general rule for exposure is that the individual should stay in the situation until his/her fear has substantially decreased and, on subsequent occasions, the individual moves up in the hierarchy to a more feared stimulus. Exposure to the feared stimulus is referred to as *flooding.*

As an example of exposure therapy or flooding, a woman who had avoided bridges for years was asked to imagine herself crossing bridges. With each repetition of this image, the therapist asked her to imagine longer bridges. (You can see that we are doing shaping here.) In this manner we construct a stimulus hierarchy of more and more difficult bridges to cross. The therapist then assigned shorter bridges for her to drive across, and later followed this with longer bridges. Repetitions of this exposure and moving up the hierarchy eliminated her fear of bridges.

Schedules of reinforcement. Reinforcements or punishments may be applied continuously (that is, 100 percent of the time that a behavior occurs it is followed by reinforcement or punishment) or intermittently (whenever consequences result less than 100 percent of the time). Ferster and Skinner (1957) have identified a variety of reinforcement schedules that depend on the frequency, timing, or ratio of behavior to reinforcements. Thus, you can be reinforced frequently or almost never, immediately or much later, and the reinforcement may or may not depend on the number of responses that you provide.

More important for our consideration is the *partial reinforcement effect* (PRE). This refers to the fact that behavior based on intermittent reinforcement (less than 100 percent reinforcement) is more difficult to extinguish than behavior based on continuous (or 100 percent) reinforcement. For example, imagine that you are reinforced only 10 percent of the time. Now I have decided to stop reinforcing you completely. (You are now on extinction.) According to the partial reinforcement effect (PRE), you might continue to respond for a very long time. In contrast, if I had been reinforcing you 100 percent of the time (continuous reinforcement), and then I stop reinforcing you (extinction), you should quickly stop responding. Behavior that has been under partial reinforcement is more difficult to extinguish than behavior that has been under continuous reinforcement.

Presumably, the partial reinforcement effect is due to the individual's greater difficulty in discriminating the reinforcement phase from the extinction phase when behavior has been established on an intermittent reinforcement schedule. With partial reinforcement followed by extinction, the individual does not realize he is no longer being reinforced; he simply believes that he has to continue responding for a long time.

For example, let us assume that the child is reinforced with praise every time he helps with the dishes (acquisition phase of learning). However, now the mother stops praising him (extinction phase). Since he has gone from 100 percent reinforcement to 0 percent reinforcement, he immediately knows he is no longer receiving reinforcement. Consequently, his dish-washing should drop off rapidly.

In contrast, let us imagine another child who is reinforced with praise 25 percent of the time that he helps with dishes. If the mother stops reinforcing him, he does not know immediately that he is not being reinforced. As far as he is concerned, he is not reinforced most of the time. Consequently, it will take longer for him to recognize that extinction has begun and therefore his behavior will persist for a longer period of time. This is referred to as the *partial reinforcement effect* (PRE).

PRE is important when we wish to fade out the reinforcing agent. For example, the teacher cannot always be there to reinforce the child. A desirable sequence of phases might be 100 percent (continuous) reinforcement during early acquisition, changing to partial reinforcement (25 percent of the time), and eventually changing to self-reinforcement. Fade-out of reinforcement and the transition to self-reinforcement are important in assuring both continued improvement and generalization of effects outside the initial learning situation.

BEHAVIORAL TECHNIQUES FOR DEPRESSION

Thus far, we have been discussing general principles of behavior modification. The cognitive-behavioral model of depression is partly based on the view that depression is a consequence of decreased activity, decreased rewards, and decreased self-reinforcement. The cognitive-behavioral therapist utilizes self-monitoring of pleasure and mastery, reward menus, and evaluation of anti-pleasure thoughts. Assisting the patient in overcoming procrastination is essential in modifying the reward opportunities. These are some of the behavioral techniques used specifically with depressed patients.

Activity Scheduling

An essential cause of depression is the lack of rewarding experiences (Lewinsohn and Gotlib 1995). In the cognitive approach, we use a wide range of behavioral techniques to increase positive mood by increasing pleasure and mastery and decreasing unpleasant, repetitive, or boring activities. The depressed patient often enters therapy complaining of a low level of activity and the inability to enjoy previously pleasurable behaviors. However, the therapist can assist the patient in identifying variations in moods associated with activity so he may learn how to plan and carry out positive activities on a daily basis.

1. Self-Monitoring Pleasure and Mastery

The therapist asks the patient to describe a typical day, from waking to sleeping. What does the patient do each hour? How much pleasure and mastery are associated with each activity? In using the scale for pleasure and mastery, the therapist may rate 10 for the greatest pleasure the patient can imagine and 0 as the absence of pleasure. Similarly, mastery is defined as feeling competent or effective in accomplishing something. Again, both ends of the scale are defined for the patient. The various degrees of mastery and pleasure are also defined using typical activities she may have experienced in the past. (The use of past and present activities is important since currently she may not be experiencing high levels of pleasure and mastery.)

Depressed patients often complain that they really are doing nothing and, therefore, they have nothing to put on the schedule. The therapist will point out that sitting alone or watching television is also an activity and represents a choice that the patient makes. Even sitting and ruminating is an activity and needs to be listed and evaluated. Indeed, rumination (obsessively reviewing one's thoughts and feelings) is highly predictive of depression (Nolen-Hoecksema 1987).

The patient is told that the purpose of monitoring pleasure and mastery is to evaluate how moods might vary with time of day and activities. This will then be used to establish activity schedules to increase pleasure and mastery.

We prefer to focus initially on the positives rather than the variation of negatives. Specifically, we do not focus on various degrees of depression or displeasure. If the patient learns that he or she has more or less depression depending on activities, it does not imply more or less pleasure. People would generally prefer viewing themselves as gaining greater pleasure rather than lessening depression. We see this as the difference between positive and negative tracking.

2. Pleasure-Predicting

According to Beck, the depressed individual has a negative triad—of self, experience, and the future. Consequently, he or she is likely to predict that activities will be low in pleasure and mastery and will use these predictions to justify avoiding the activities. As a result, the patient will have fewer rewarding experiences, thereby maintaining the depression and the negative triad.

Activity schedules may be used to assess the patient's negative predictions. The patient is given an activity schedule (see Table 5–2) and asked to indicate for each hour any planned activities over the next few days (or week, if the patient is seen once a week). For each planned activity, the patient is asked to indicate how much pleasure and mastery he expects. On a separate activity schedule, the patient will keep a list of the actual activities and how much pleasure and mastery were

Table 5–2. Activity Schedule: Monday A.M. (Predicted)

Time	Activity	P = Pleasure	M = Mastery
6:00	A.M.		
7:00	Wake, Shower	P = 2	M = 0
8:00	Breakfast, Travel to Work	P = 1	M = 0
9:00	Work on Account	P = 0	M = 1
10:00	Make Calls, Work on Account	P = 0	M = 1
11:00	Meeting	P = 1	M = 0
12:00	Lunch	P = 2	M = 0

really obtained. Consider the following activity schedule of an accountant:

Examination of this patient's activity schedule indicates very low predictions for Monday morning. The patient is then asked to keep track of the actual outcome to see if his predictions were valid. (See Table 5–3 for the actual activity schedule.)

Although the actual levels of pleasure and mastery were not very high, they were higher than the patient expected. This difference is presented to the patient.

Therapist: You can see that your predictions of pleasure and mastery were somewhat lower than the actual pleasure and mastery. What do you make of that?

Table 5–3. Activity Schedule: Monday A.M. (Actual)

Time	Activity	P = Pleasure	M = Mastery
6:00	A.M.		
7:00	Wake, Shower	P = 3	M = 2
8:00	Breakfast, Travel to Work	P = 3	M = 2
9:00	Work on Account	P = 3	M = 4
10:00	Make Calls, Work on Account	P = 3	M = 4
11:00	Meeting	P = 4	M = 4
12:00	Lunch	P = 3	M = 2

Patient: I guess I'm inclined to underestimate how good things will be.

Therapist: What is the consequence for you if you do that?

Patient: I guess I end up doing less.

Therapist: And what is the consequence of doing less?

Patient: Then I stay depressed.

Therapist: So, by making negative predictions you decrease your activity level and maintain your depression.

3. Assigning Activities

The goal of behavioral interventions is to increase positive and decrease negative behavior. But which positive activities can be assigned to the patient? The menu of positive activities is derived from three sources. First, which current activities are highly rated by the patient? For example, if the patient gives high ratings to interacting with friends, then these behaviors may be assigned for the next week. Specifically, the patient agrees that he will schedule time with friends over the next week and record these pleasure ratings. Second, which activities prior to the depressive episode were enjoyable? Since depression is marked by a decrease in previously rewarding activities, such rewarding activities can be assigned. For example, if the patient used to exercise and enjoy it, then exercise can be made a homework assignment. What was once enjoyable has a good chance of being enjoyable again. However, current enjoyment may be undermined by negative thoughts regarding previous activity. (We will discuss this later.) And third, are there any activities that the patient has always wanted to do, but has never tried? For example, one patient who was going through a divorce had always wanted to take an art course but never did. Simply planning this new activity lifted her mood.

Activity scheduling is useful in increasing a sense of self-

efficacy and in overcoming short-term and long-term hopelessness. Self-efficacy is increased by empowering the patient
to obtain rewards on his or her own. Hopelessness is challenged by showing the patient that his or her mood may be
modified by engaging in activities now and by planning more
challenging goals for the future.

4. Examining Negative Thoughts
   Related to Inactivity

The clinician wants to assign activities with a high likelihood of
being carried out. Consequently, it is important to increase the
difficulty level of the activities assigned gradually. The overly
ambitious therapist may inadvertently undermine the patient's progress by expecting too much change in behavior. As
with all behavioral and cognitive assignments, it is important
to provide the patient with specific goals; for example, "visit
with *two* friends," rather than "see more friends this week."
The perfectionistic and self-critical patient might end up seeing
three friends but believe that she has failed because a friend
was not seen every day.

Each homework assignment contains a cognitive element.
The patient who carries out an activity such as going to a party
but reports a low level of pleasure may be asked why it
resulted in such low pleasure. For example, the patient may
use self-comparisons to discount the activity: "I used to enjoy
this more in the past when I wasn't depressed." Or the patient
may have set unrealistic goals: "I didn't meet anyone to have a
relationship with." The therapist should consider it an experiment: "What did you learn from carrying out this activity?"

5. Low-Reward Activities

A common correlate of depression is engaging in low-reward
activities that are isolating and non-energetic. For example,

watching television or sitting home alone ruminating are low-reward, non-energetic activities that result in depression and provide no access to other positive rewards. In examining the activity schedule, the therapist will evaluate the content of low-reward or low-mastery activities, pointing out the difference in pleasure ratings between low- and high-reward behaviors.

Therapist: You gave yourself low ratings of 2 for watching television, but you gave yourself higher ratings of 6 for having lunch with your friend. What do you make of this?

By illustrating the contrast between moods for different activities, the patient learns that he can modify his mood simply by changing activities.

Recently, Nolen-Hoecksema (1987) indicated that people who engage in rumination are far more likely to get depressed, stay depressed, and have relapses of depression. Rumination is the act of passively sitting around and asking oneself rhetorical questions ("Why does this happen to me?"), self-absorption with emotions and bodily sensations ("I just feel lousy," "I've got so many aches and pains"), and generally complaining. Ruminators are contrasted with people who are instrumental or resourceful—people who are willing to engage in activities, take advice on how to change themselves, distract themselves from their negativity, and tolerate frustration. Quite often, the passive patient who reports a low level of activity is engaged in rumination. The therapist can determine if the patient is ruminating by asking him what is going through his mind when he is inactive. The patient may keep a diary of these thoughts.

Ruminative thoughts seldom lead to a satisfactory answer. For example, "Why am I always having problems?" is a thought that seldom yields a useful answer. These ruminative thoughts can be replaced by a personal empowerment or self-efficacy question, such as "What can I do right now that will be rewarding?" By focusing on thoughts that lead to behavior, rather than to more self-preoccupation and remorse, the patient can be assisted in interrupting this depressive cognitive style.

6. Increasing Choice of Behaviors

After the therapist has contrasted low- and high-reward activities, she may examine the patient's evaluations of costs and benefits of the low-reward behavior. For example, staying home and watching TV may be preferred because of the low risk of rejection.

Patient: If I were to go to a party on Saturday night, I'd probably be rejected and I'd see that everyone else was having a great time and I was all alone.

Since the patient has gathered information on activities during the first two weeks of therapy, we now have some evidence that there are behaviors leading to higher rewards. Further, the patient may examine his reward menu (past or anticipated positive behaviors) and consider those behaviors as alternatives to the low-reward behaviors.

Therapist: I can see that watching TV was a low-reward behavior. Perhaps you could consider other behaviors on your reward list that have higher ratings. What are the costs and benefits of this low-reward behavior compared with the costs and benefits of these other two behaviors?

7. Procrastination

Depressed patients often procrastinate on behavioral assignments. The inexperienced therapist may use this as an opportunity to lecture the patient or challenge her motivation to change. As a result, the patient will feel criticized and dominated and use this as more evidence of what a failure she is. We recommend using each failure as an opportunity to collect information.

Therapist: Let's see. You planned to go to a concert on Saturday night but decided to stay home instead. Let's examine what was going through your mind at the time. Try to imagine yourself on Saturday when you were considering going to the concert. What were you thinking?

Patient: I thought "I'll just have another lousy time. I won't meet anyone."

Therapist: I see. And if you didn't meet anyone, then what would that make you think?

Patient: Oh, I'd just think: "This proves what a loser I am."

Therapist: So, you would conclude that you were a loser if you went to a concert and didn't meet anyone?

Patient: Yeah.

In the foregoing example, the reason the patient avoids the concert is that his self-esteem is at stake—if he goes and does not meet anyone, that will prove he is a loser. This underlying assumption may then be used for further cognitive interventions on his need for approval and his need for a guarantee. It is these assumptions that undermine his activity scheduling.

The therapist may challenge that assumption by expanding the goals for going to the concert.

Therapist: Are there any other goals you could aim for in going to a concert?

Patient: I could go to hear the music or to get out of the apartment—or to stop thinking about my problems for a while.

The patient's need for certainty may be challenged.

Therapist: It sounded like to make it worthwhile you needed to know for sure that you would meet someone. Are you trying to attain certainty or increase probability? What would be the costs and benefits of demanding certainty before you go? What would be the costs and benefits of simply trying to increase the probability of meeting someone?

8. Low Frustration Tolerance and Inactivity

Inactivity is often associated with the belief that one should not engage in activity unless one is first motivated—motivation leads to activity. This is a widely held, common-sense view that when applied to depressed people results in greater inactivity. The patient's belief may be challenged by using the activity schedule to chart "motivation to be active." Is the motivation higher or lower following activities? What would happen if she engaged in an activity when she had low motivation? The patient might predict that she would feel overwhelmed or greatly fatigued. These predictions may be tested using the activity schedule, measuring feelings of "being overwhelmed" before and after activities are carried out. Generally, the patient's feelings of being "overwhelmed" and "fatigued" are the result of feeling apprehensive about the activity, not the result of the activity itself. In fact, it would be expected that the patient would feel less overwhelmed and less fatigued after the activity.

6

COGNITIVE INTERVENTIONS

INITIAL ASSESSMENT

When the adult patient presents for evaluation and treatment, the clinician cannot rely on the patient's self-evaluation. We require the patient at our initial intake to complete a variety of self-report forms that assess depression (Beck Depression Inventory (BDI)), anxiety (Beck Anxiety Inventory (BAI)), symptom clusters assessing anxiety, depression, phobia, psychoticism, paranoia, and somatization (SCL 90R), and personality disorder (SCID II). Some clinicians—especially those working in medical settings—may use the Structured Clinical Interview (SCID) to assesses *DSM-III-R* disorders in a methodical, programmatic way. We find that when the patient has been evaluated by the SCID, there is a greater likelihood of more than one diagnosis. For example, such evaluations may reveal major depressive episode, recurrent dysthymia, panic disorder with agoraphobia, and alcohol abuse. One can argue that all patients should be given this test, but clinicians may be either hesitant to require such an extensive interview or may themselves lack training with the SCID. We would recommend that all clinicians familiarize themselves with the structure of the SCID so that they can at least be aware of the kinds of questions that should be asked during the initial interview.

The SCID II, developed by Spitzer and colleagues (1992) at Columbia University Medical School, is a useful screening device for Axis II (personality disorder). The patient completes a questionnaire that assesses the major personality disorders. The clinician should follow up the questions on the SCID II with a more detailed evaluation in order to assess which, if any, of the personality disorders merit diagnosis.

The most commonly used self-report evaluation for depression is the Beck Depression Inventory (BDI). This twenty-one-item questionnaire can be filled out by patients at the intake and at all subsequent sessions. Each item yields a score ranging from 0 to 3, with a maximum total score ranging from 0 to 63. The mean score in the non-clinical population is 6. Arbitrary cutoffs for various ranges of depression are 0–10 (non-depressed), 11–15 (mild depression), 16–20 (moderate depression), 21–30 (high level of depression), above 30 (severe depression). The BDI contains a variety of symptom clusters, including self-criticism, and affective, hopeless, vegetative, cognitive, and interpersonal symptoms. The clinician can also use the Hamilton to evaluate the patient's general presentation of depression and any psychotic elements such as delusions (Hamilton 1960). The Hamilton Rating Scale for Depression includes 24 items (e. g., mood, guilt, suicidality, insomnia), with the clinician rating the patient on a 5-point scale (0–4).

In addition to the BDI, the Symptom Checklist 90R (SCL 90R) is used to evaluate a variety of other symptom factors. This 90-item self-report questionnaire allows the clinician to evaluate several symptom factors: depression, phobic anxiety, psychoticism, somatic complaints, interpersonal sensitivity, and hostility. Supplementing these forms, the clinician may also use the SCID and the SCID II. While the SCID is often used in research settings and requires a personal interview of some length, we have found that we can bypass the formal application of the SCID in clinical practice if we attend to important questions in all intake interviews. We view it as essential that the clinician inquire about alcohol and drug abuse, history of manic episodes, eating disorders, unusual dietary styles, sleep deprivation, prescription drugs, organic symptoms, and history of major depressive episode. In addition, the clinician should ascertain if the depression is secondary to other problems, such as panic disorder and agoraphobia. The SCID II (Spitzer et al. 1992) is useful for screening personality disorders (Axis II) and can direct the clinician to further inquiry about specific Axis II problems.

For patients who are married or cohabiting, we recommend the Locke-Wallace Marital Adjustment Test (1959). This is a simple self-report form that assesses general level of satisfaction in the marriage, points of disagreement, regret over commitment, and the willingness of the patient to confide in his or her partner. Scores below 100 are problematic, tending to predict marital dissatisfaction and divorce. In addition to the Locke-Wallace, patients may also complete specific self-report forms that assess beliefs about marriage, communication style, and sexual behavior.

Specific Axis I disorders may be assessed with other self-report forms. For example, the Fear Questionnaire allows the clinician to assess agoraphobia and social phobia, the Yale-Brown Obsessive-Compulsive Questionnaire assesses a variety of obsessions, compulsions, and other rituals, and there are other self-report questionnaires that allow us to assess alcohol and drug abuse (see Donovan and Marlatt 1988).

Self-report forms are valuable for a number of reasons. First, they are easy to administer; patients can be sent these forms to fill out before they arrive for their first session. Second, they can be easily scored—in one to five minutes. Third, they are based on empirically derived norms, allowing us to compare the patient's score with the scores of others. Fourth, they allow continual measurement throughout therapy so that we can assess, for example, how much depression has changed, which symptoms have changed, and what still needs to be modified. Given the ever-growing influence of managed care, with its demand for evaluation throughout therapy, it seems inevitable that assessment will move more toward these standardized evaluations. Self-report forms do not replace the individual interview, but they do provide the interviewer with a considerable data base for the patient.

Cognitive Assessment

The cognitive therapy intake is different from traditional intake interviews. The therapist is not only interested in the patient's symptoms and life history but also in his interpretations of events. For example, the patient may report that he felt depressed and hopeless after the breakup of a relationship and that these feelings precipitated the current major depressive episode. The therapist will inquire as to the meaning of the breakup.

Therapist: You said you felt depressed and hopeless after you and Susan broke up. I am going to give you some sentences and I want you to finish them with the first thoughts that come to mind. "I felt depressed when we broke up because I thought . . ."

Patient: . . . I'll never be able to be with her again.

Therapist: And if I can never be with her again I feel depressed because I think . . .

Patient: I can never be happy with anyone else.

The cognitive assessment attempts to elicit the patient's idiosyncratic interpretations of events. Unfortunately many clinicians believe they know what the event meant to the patient, but they may be completely wrong. For example, different patients might become depressed because the breakup signifies that they are unlovable, that they will not be able to take care of themselves, or that they cannot trust their judgment. The patient's interpretation is key, for it will become one of the initial targets for therapy.

The cognitive therapist will try to elicit automatic thoughts, which are thoughts that come spontaneously, seem plausible to the patient, and are associated with negative affect. Typical automatic thoughts are "I'll never be happy" or "I'll lose control" or "I'm a failure." More general, pervasive thoughts are called underlying assumptions: these refer to "should statements" (e.g., "I should get the approval of everyone") and "if–then statements" (e.g., "If I don't get approval, then I'm a failure").

Many patients—especially anxious patients—report having visual images when they are anxious. These are not hallucinations, but rather images that often entail the belief that something dangerous will happen. For example, a panic disorder patient had the image that she would be driving across a bridge, lose control, and see herself plummeting to her death. Positive images are often instructive because they indicate the patient's belief about how problems might be satisfactorily resolved. When the therapist asked a 45-year-old single woman what positive visual image she could produce, she began to describe herself in a bedroom holding a man she loved. This then elicited crying because she believed this would never happen. A 62-year-old married woman, reporting almost forty years of marital discord and dysthymia, had the "positive" image of her husband and herself driving on the highway, getting into an accident where she is thrown free, while he is killed. This dramatic image was positive for her: "At last I would be free of him . . . and I would not have to make any decisions." Interestingly, her image allowed her to "kill" her husband without taking responsibility for her own hostility.

In a later chapter we will discuss how the therapist can elicit automatic thoughts and underlying assumptions and help the patient evaluate them. Although some may believe that cognitive therapy involves the power of positive thinking, this is an incorrect evaluation. Many automatic thoughts may be true—for example, the individual may predict that he will be rejected or fail the exam—and he may be right. The question to be addressed is, "If you are rejected at the party, what would that *mean* to you?" The patient might respond that the future will be filled with other rejections.

TESTING AUTOMATIC THOUGHTS

Automatic thoughts occur spontaneously, seem plausible to the patient, and are associated with negative affect. We can say that automatic thoughts are assessments or interpretations of events. They are stipulations or propositions: "I'll never be happy again," "I am a failure," or "It's all my fault." They may be either true or false. Automatic thoughts are distinguished from feelings or emotions—such as sadness, anxiety, fear, or hopelessness. Feelings or emotions have the same status as sensations; they are indisputable. For example, it would make little sense to say, "Even though you feel anxious, you are not anxious." The therapist does not test or challenge whether the patient has these feelings: rather, she examines the thoughts that give rise to the feelings. For example, "I feel sad because I *think* I'll never succeed at anything." The therapist assists the patient in examining the proposition, "I'll never succeed at anything."

Consider the following: you are walking along a dark alley in the city and you hear the footsteps of two large men coming from behind. How do you *feel?* Your feeling—anxiety, indifference, or even elation—will depend on your interpretation of the meaning of these footsteps. You might have the thought, "I'm going to be mugged!" which will lead to the feeling of fear and the behavior of escape. Or you could think, "It's just two businessmen leaving a restaurant," in which case you will have a feeling of indifference and your behavior will remain the same—you will continue your walk. Or you could have the interpretation that these are friends of yours from the psychology convention, in which case your feeling will be pleasure, and your behavior might be to turn around and try to join them. The point is that the same situation may give rise to any number of thoughts and feelings. The question is, "Which thought is valid?"

To determine which thought is valid requires examining the evidence and your reasoning. For example, you could examine the evidence by turning around and seeing who is behind you. Cognitive therapy largely consists in the elicitation and examination of the automatic thoughts and assumptions that people display when they are feeling anxious, depressed, or angry. The negative thoughts of the patient may be categorized into the following distortions:

Cognitive Distortions

1. Mind reading: You assume you know what people think without having sufficient evidence of their thoughts. "He thinks I'm a loser."

2. Fortune telling: You predict the future; things will get worse or there is danger ahead. "I'll fail that exam" and "I won't get the job."

3. Catastrophizing: You believe that what has happened or will happen is so awful and unbearable that you won't be able to stand it. "It would be terrible if I failed."

4. Labeling: You assign global negative traits to yourself and others. "I'm undesirable" or "He's a rotten person."

5. Discounting positives: You claim that the positives you or others attain are trivial: "That's what wives are supposed to do, so it doesn't count when she's nice to me." "Those successes were easy, so they don't matter."

6. Negative filter: You focus almost exclusively on the negatives and seldom notice the positives. "Look at all the people who don't like me."

7. Overgeneralizing: You perceive a global pattern of negatives on the basis of a single incident. "This generally happens to me. I seem to fail at a lot of things."

8. Dichotomous thinking: You view events or people in all-or-nothing terms. "I get rejected by everyone" or "It was a waste of time."

9. Shoulds: You interpret events in terms of how things should be rather than simply focusing on what is. "I should do well. If I don't, then I'm a failure."

10. Personalizing: You assign a disproportionate amount of blame to yourself for negative happenings and fail to see that certain events are also caused by others. "The marriage ended because I failed."

11. Blaming: You focus on the other person as the source of your negative feelings, and you refuse to take responsibility for changing yourself. "She's to blame for the way I feel now" or "My parents caused all my problems."

12. Unfair comparisons: You interpret events in terms of standards that are unrealistic; for example, you focus primarily on others who do better than you and find yourself inferior by comparison. "She's more successful than I am" or "Others did better than I on the test."

13. Regret orientation: You focus on the idea that you could have done better in the past, rather than on what you can do better now. "I could have had a better job if I had tried" or "I shouldn't have said that."

14. What if? You keep asking a series of questions about "what if" something happens and fail to be satisfied with any of the answers. "Yeah, but what if I get anxious? Or what if I can't catch my breath?"

15. Emotional reasoning: You let your feelings guide your interpretation of reality; "I feel depressed, therefore my marriage is not working out."

16. Inability to disconfirm: You reject any evidence or arguments that might contradict your negative thoughts. When you think "I'm unlovable," you reject as irrelevant any evidence that people like you. Consequently, your thought cannot be refuted: "That's not the real issue. There are deeper problems. There are other factors."

17. Judgment focus: You view yourself, others, and events in terms of evaluations of good–bad or superior–inferior, rather than simply describing, accepting, or understanding. You are continually measuring yourself and others according to arbitrary standards, finding that you and others fall short. You are focused on the judgments of others as well as your own judgments of yourself. "I didn't perform well in college" or "If I take up tennis, I won't do well" or "Look how successful she is. I'm not successful."

TESTING AND CHALLENGING AUTOMATIC THOUGHTS

In evaluating and testing automatic thoughts and maladaptive assumptions or rules, the therapist may be guided by a set of questions he can pose to the patient.

What if the automatic thought is true?   The therapist should keep in mind that some automatic thoughts may be partly or even largely true. Cognitive therapy is not the power of positive thinking or simply the refutation of every negative belief that the patient has. When automatic thoughts are true, then the therapist may determine if behavioral changes are indicated or if the patient's underlying assumptions need to be modified. For example, a woman who had been depressed for more than two years since she was fired had the automatic thought that she interviewed very poorly. The therapist and the patient collected information about her interviews and, indeed, she had been rejected at every one of them. The therapist then engaged her in a behavioral rehearsal where she practiced her interview with the therapist during the session. It was immediately apparent that she was correct—she appeared defensive, self-absorbed, and too eager to make an impression.

Therapist: It appears that your automatic thought is valid. You do come across poorly in the interview.
Patient: See, it's just as I expected. I'll never get a job.
Therapist: No, actually this was a great discovery. We now know exactly what you have to change in order to get a job. We now have to design good interviewing skills.

The therapist and the patient developed behavioral targets for interviewing, a list of do's and don'ts that she practiced at home using a tape recorder and rehearsed in session with the therapist. On her next two interviews she was offered jobs and now, ten years later, she has been continuously employed in a highly competitive job.

The therapist should not rely on one or two challenges to a thought, since the automatic thought may have been practiced for decades. We recommend focusing on just a few central automatic thoughts per session, utilizing a variety of techniques on each thought. The following are commonly effective challenges to automatic thoughts:

TWELVE QUESTIONS TO ASK ABOUT AN AUTOMATIC THOUGHT

1. Which cognitive distortion are you using? Are you engaging in labeling, all-or-nothing thinking, catastrophizing?

2. How much do you believe in this thought?

3. What are the advantages and disadvantages of this thought?

4. What is the evidence for and against this thought?

5. What is the quality of the evidence you are using? Could you convince a jury that your negative interpretation is the best or only valid one?

6. What if the thought is true? Why would that bother you?

7. Even if the thought is true, could you think of other positive behaviors that you might engage in despite this?

8. If someone else had this problem, what advice would you give him?

9. If someone else had this problem, would you judge him as negatively as you judge yourself? Why or why not?

10. How many times in the past have you had this kind of thought? Have you ever been wrong?

11. Is there something you could do to determine if this thought is true?

12. If the thought is true, are there some things you can do to improve the situation?

Examples of Specific Challenges

It is beyond the scope of this book to provide the clinician with an exhaustive list of challenges to all automatic thoughts. However, the following are useful questions to ask about specific cognitive distortions:

Mind reading: "She probably thinks I'm a loser"

Examine the evidence. Are you basing this on a guess or on a fact?

Why would that be so bad? Do you conclude that because she doesn't like you there is something defective about you? Could it be that people have different tastes?

Challenge the need for approval. Does your self-worth depend on obtaining the approval of everyone? Is anyone approved by everyone? No matter what you do, you can't please everyone. Even if someone doesn't like you, aren't there positive behaviors that are still within your control?

Are there other people who do like you? Are you focusing on the few people who don't like you and not considering the others who do like you? Is it possible to like yourself regardless of what someone else thinks of you?

Catastrophizing: "It would be awful if I was rejected."

Continuum technique: If 100 percent corresponds to the worst thing imaginable (e.g., nuclear holocaust) and 0 percent corresponds to the absence of anything negative, where would you put this event in Figure 6–1? Fill in every 10 percent on the scale.

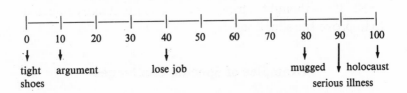

Figure 6–1. Continuum Technique: Negative Events

Exactly what will happen? If you were rejected, what specific events would be upsetting? What would *not* happen; what would not change in your life? What would you still be able to do even if it were true?

What's the best, worst, and most probable outcome? Could anything positive happen? For example, is it possible that you might be accepted—by this person or someone else? Is it useful to learn that you can tolerate rejection? What is the worst thing that could happen if this person did not like you? What is the most probable prediction about people liking you?

Past history of predictions: Do you tend to make many negative predictions? Do most or all of them fail to come true? Is there any reason to believe that this is just another negative prediction that will not come true?

> *Fortune telling:* "I will fail."

What is the evidence? Are you basing this prediction on any reasonable evidence? Is there any evidence that you might succeed? Is your standard of success too high? If you do well on part of the task, do you give yourself credit for that?

What advantage is there in assuming the worst? What are the costs and benefits of your predicting the worst? Do you think pessimism prepares you for the worst?

Past predictions: How many false alarms have you had? Do you generally make negative predictions that do not come true?

What could be the best, worst, most probable outcome? Is it possible that the most probable outcome is somewhere between the worst and the best? Are there any other outcomes that you have yet to consider?

How could you cope with the outcome? If you did fail at this task, are there resources and behaviors available to help you cope?

> *Labeling:* "I'm a failure."

Contrast behaviors with persons. Is it a behavior that fails or the entire person?

Is there any variation in the behavior? Is there any evidence that some of your behaviors are rewarded? Are there other sources of reward in your life?

How does this compare with norms? What is the norm for this behavior? Are there people above and below you on this performance scale? Does your performance move up and down in the distribution—are you sometimes better than at other times?

Double standard technique: If someone else performed as you have, would you consider her a failure? Why not? What is the rationale of holding yourself to a higher standard than you use for others?

Are you discounting your positives? Are you not giving yourself proper credit for some good things you have accomplished? What is the rationale for that?

Can you keep track over the next week of positive experiences and mastery? When you monitor your positives during the week, are you surprised that there are some? What would happen if you gave yourself credit for these positives?

Personalizing: "It's all my fault."

List positives and negatives for each person. What was the contribution for each person in the event? List them and rate their importance.

Use a pie chart to divide responsibility. Using the information from the previous question, design a pie chart indicating the relative contributions to the event.

Would others have done better, worse? Was this an unusually difficult task? Would everyone else have done better than you?

What could you do differently in the future? Even if you were a major contributor to the negative outcome, is there anything you could learn from this to improve yourself in the future? How could you turn this into a learning experience?

Unfair comparisons: "She did better than I did."

Examine the range and variability of the normal distribution. Consider the test you took. What was the range of scores on the test and what was the norm? Where do you stand in comparison with the range?

What is the logic of comparing yourself against an extreme? Do you assume that you should do better than everyone else? Are you a perfectionist? Why do you expect superior behavior from yourself?

Are you comparing behaviors, but inferring personal worth? Performance is a measure of a behavior, not a person. Are you assuming that your specific behavior in this specific situation is a measure of your value as a person?

What would you think of someone who did worse than you? Would you be as critical of others who do less well than you? Imagine criticizing a friend who does less well. How does it sound to you?

Differentiate other positive qualities of self. Is self-worth focused on only one set of behaviors? Rather than focus on this one performance, can you consider a variety of other areas where you do well or find satisfaction? What if you were to focus your concern and energy on these other areas?

> *Inability to disconfirm:* "That's not relevant to whether I'm a failure."

How would you define the negative construct? Can you give a clear and concise definition of what a failure is? Is it at all possible to collect information relevant to this concept?

How would you define the positive construct? What is the opposite of your construct of failure? Is it success? Complete success? Can you give a clear and concise definition of what success is?

Is there any evidence of positive behaviors? Are there examples of any positive behaviors related to your construct? Do these offer even partial disconfirmation of your construct?

Examine the degree and frequency of positive behaviors. How often and to what extent do you engage in positives? Neutrals? Negatives? Make a pie chart to examine the relative importance of the negatives.

Use point–counterpoint technique. Consider challenging *both* the negative thoughts and rational responses. Perhaps there is an underlying assumption that makes it difficult to disconfirm your negative beliefs. For example, consider the following:

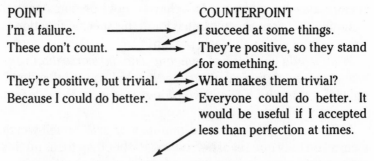

POINT   COUNTERPOINT

I'm a failure.   I succeed at some things.

These don't count.   They're positive, so they stand for something.

They're positive, but trivial.   What makes them trivial?

Because I could do better.   Everyone could do better. It would be useful if I accepted less than perfection at times.

If I accept less than perfection, I'll become mediocre (underlying assumption).

The underlying thought, "If I accept less than perfection, then I'm mediocre," is the resistant assumption. This patient's perfectionism leads her to refuse to disconfirm her negative evaluations of herself because she believes this will lead her to accept mediocrity. She views perfectionism as the only motivational factor that keeps her from slipping into mediocrity. Later in this chapter we will describe some methods that can be used in testing and challenging these underlying rules—the maladaptive assumptions that create the vulnerability to depression and anxiety.

SPECIFIC AFFECT AND AUTOMATIC THOUGHTS

The cognitive model proposes that different emotions are often associated with specific cognitive content and specific automatic thought distortions. In this section, I describe typical cognitive content and examples of automatic thoughts for depression, anxiety, and anger.

Depression

Content: Loss, failure, negative view of self, experience, and future

Typical automatic thoughts
Labeling: I'm a failure.
Fortune telling: I'll always be unhappy.
Personalizing: Everyone else is doing well except me.
Maximization: My failure is enormous.

In the case of depression, the patient's thoughts are focused on loss, failure, and a negative view of the future. He predicts that he will fail, he believes he will never be happy, and he thinks everyone else is successful. For example, a very successful and wealthy investor believed he could not concentrate, that he was a failure because he had made "only $1 million in profits the previous year." He measured this against prior years of $3-to-$4 million and predicted that he was headed for financial collapse.

(I offer this example because it so clearly illustrates how distorted and extreme depressive thinking can be and how exaggerated social comparisons often underlie negative self-esteem.)

Anxiety

Content: Danger, imminent threat, uncertainty

Typical automatic thoughts

Labeling: I'm going crazy.
Fortune telling: I'll lose control.
Catastrophizing: It would be awful if I seemed anxious.
What if: What if I freeze and can't talk?

The anxious patient focuses on danger to himself, either external danger of being humiliated or failing or internal danger from his anxiety symptoms. For example, a young man, who had an inner-ear problem associated with dizziness, would become dizzy at his job as a bartender because it required his moving around quickly. His automatic thoughts were: "Something terrible is happening to me. I will faint and collapse to the floor. People will think I'm weak and inferior. I can't stand people thinking that of me."

Anger

Content: Shoulds, retaliation

Typical automatic thoughts
Labeling: He's rotten to have done that to me.
Personalizing: She's trying to get me angry.
Shoulds: He shouldn't have done that. I should get back at him.
Catastrophizing: I can't stand it when she says that.

The angry patient is focused on thoughts of rule violation, provocation, and retaliation. An angry husband claimed that he would not participate in therapy homework because he wanted his wife to get better before he would make the investment. His thoughts were, "She should have gotten better before. I'm not going to give her what she wants until she proves to me it's worth it. I just can't stand the way she's been."

As the foregoing illustrates, there is different content in the automatic thoughts and assumptions of patients who are depressed, anxious, or angry. The therapist needs to elicit a variety of automatic thoughts in order to determine the idiosyncratic meaning of events for patients. We should never assume that because patients are depressed, we know why they are depressed. On the contrary, they know why they are depressed and they need help in uncovering their negative automatic thoughts and assumptions.

The cognitive therapist focuses on the immediate, conscious, and accessible automatic thoughts that are associated with negative feelings and behavior. Unlike the psychodynamic therapist who may make his own interpretation of what the patient is really thinking, the cognitive therapist is interested in the patient's idiosyncratic process of thinking. The therapist collaborates with the patient in eliciting and testing these negative thoughts. Should the thoughts prove to be accurate, the patient may learn new behaviors to cope with the situation or change it.

Automatic thoughts are the first line of cognitive inquiry. The underlying assumptions or the patient's rules for interpretation are the second level of inquiry. For example, if the patient predicts that he will fail at a task, it is the assumption "I should never fail" or "I am a failure if I fail" or "People will think less of me if I fail" that makes the patient vulnerable to situational determinants of depression, anxiety, and anger.

TESTING ASSUMPTIONS

As already indicated, automatic thoughts derive their potential for negative affect because of the patient's underlying maladaptive assumptions. The individual who predicts that someone will not like him is not likely to be upset unless he overvalues being liked; for example, if he believes that he is worthless if someone does not like him. But how can the therapist identify these underlying assumptions and modify them through cognitive therapy?

1. Identifying Assumptions

Underlying assumptions are the rules, imperatives, shoulds, or if-then statements that guide the patient's thinking. Examples of assumptions are: "I should be perfect," "I must get other people to like me," "If someone doesn't like me, then I am inferior," or "I should succeed in everything I try." Assumptions are general and abstract, reflecting a universal and inflexible quality. They are distinguished from simple predictions, such as, "If I take the exam, I will fail."

Assumptions may be identified by using the vertical descent technique, beginning with an automatic thought and inquiring why it would be a problem if the thought were true. For example:

1. I won't do well on the exam.——>
2. If I don't do well on the exam, then I'm not that smart.——>
3. Which means I'm really stupid.

The underlying assumption is, "If I do not do well at something, then I am not smart or I am stupid." The therapist may then inquire what it would mean if the patient found out that he is stupid: "If I'm stupid, then I'm worthless" or "If I'm stupid, then people won't want to be with me." These rules determine whether the patient will feel depressed if the automatic thought is true.

2. Cost–Benefit Analysis

Many of the techniques used in challenging automatic thoughts are applicable to challenging underlying assumptions. The patient is asked to write down the assumption and indicate the degree to which he or she believes the assumption to be true (rating the assumption from 0 percent to 100 percent belief). Next, the patient lists the costs and the benefits of holding the assumption, and weighs the balance. The therapist asks if the costs and benefits are equal. Do the costs (benefits) outweigh the benefits (costs)? "If you had to divide 100 points between the costs and benefits of the assumption, how would you divide the points?" (See Table 6–1.)

The patient's assumption is contrasted with a less negative and less rigid assumption. For example, the assumption that "I should be perfect" may be contrasted with "It would be nice to do well on some things" or "It is OK to make mistakes sometimes." The patient then does a cost–benefit analysis for each contrasting adaptive assumption. (See Table 6–2.)

After the patient has weighed the costs and benefits for each assumption, he or she will examine the resultant outcome, which is defined as the benefits minus the costs. In the preceding examples, the resultant outcome for perfectionism was (-30), whereas the resultant outcome for imperfectionism was $(+60)$. Since $(+60)$ is greater than (-30), imperfectionism is the more desirable assumption for the patient.

Table 6–1. Cost–Benefits for Perfectionism

Costs	Benefits
Depression, anxiety, dissatisfaction, self-criticism, procrastination, indecision.	Motivates me to try harder and gives me a standard to measure myself against.
Costs = 65%	
Benefits = 35%	
Resultant = − 30%	

Table 6-2. Costs-Benefits for Accepting Imperfection

Costs	Benefits
I won't try as hard	I'll be less self-critical
I'll risk becoming average	I'll take pride in some things I do
	I'll be less anxious, less depressed, less procastinating, more willing to make decisions, more realistic.
Costs = 20%	Benefits = 80%
Resultant = +60%	

Each cost and benefit may be individually examined by listing the evidence for and against it. Many perfectionists believe that their perfectionism causes them to try harder. However, there may be evidence against this belief in that their perfectionism may actually result in greater procrastination and inefficient effort in pointless behavior. Do they try harder or do they try efficiently?

It is useful to ask the patient which costs and which benefits stand out as the important ones. This will help guide the therapist in further inquiry as to which ideas have been modified and which still need examination. The patient may change his ratings for costs-benefits at any time. This often occurs after the patient has examined the evidence for selected costs or benefits.

Suppose the patient decides that the perfectionist assumption is more desirable than imperfectionism. If so, the therapist will inquire about the specific rationale for this selection. Once the patient decides, the therapist may ask, "If you are deciding in favor of perfectionism, then I assume you are also saying you prefer self-criticism, anxiety, and depression to the benefits of imperfectionism." It is important to confront the patient with the implication of the assumption in order to affect the motivation to change it. Making a choice to live life by certain assumptions and values carries implications about costs and benefits. The patient needs to understand the true existential point—there is no free lunch.

3. Examining Criteria

The patient's assumption is tested by first establishing definitions for key terms. The patient is instructed that we cannot test an assumption unless we have first determined what we are talking about. For example, the assumption that "I must succeed at everything or I am a failure" can be analyzed for the definitions of "succeed," "everything," "I am" and "failure." The patient is asked for her own definitions for each term. "Succeed" may be defined as "obtaining my goals." The patient is then asked if she obtained 70 percent of her goals would this qualify as "partial success" or "no success." Often patients' definitions are reaching "all my goals at 100 percent."

The patient may be told that we want to examine his assumptions, but to do so we must first define the terms. "If we were to do a scientific study on your assumption and wanted to collect data on success, how would we know how to choose people or behaviors that are successful?" "How would you define success so that a stranger would know exactly what you were talking about?" "How would you define the opposite of success?"

Patients may be asked for denotative definitions of a concept, for example, "Could you give me some specific examples of people who are successful . . . people who are failing?" The patient's denotative examples may then be compared with others' concrete examples of success and failure.

The patient's definition that success means reaching goals would then be open to question: "How would we determine the goals—is it the individual's goals? Reasonable goals? My goals?" Internal contradictions may be pointed out once a definition is offered: "If someone sets a goal of making $10 million, but he only makes $9 million, does that imply he had no success? From your definition, he didn't reach his goal."

The patient's definitions are examined to determine if they lead to possible disconfirmation by empirical observation, or whether they qualify for the verifiability principle. Specifically, are there any realistic observations that could lead us to disconfirm a proposition? For example, defining "worthwhile" as having worth without offering any further definitions of what worth might mean reduces it to a meaningless term since it cannot be confirmed or disconfirmed. The verifiability principle is essential in testing any proposition: "How would we know if you were no longer a failure?" "How would we know if you were no longer rejected?" "What is the opposite of a failure?"

Many perfectionistic patients have idiosyncratic definitions, especially of success and failure. The patient's definitions may then be compared with how other people would define success and failure. For example, would other people define success as "superior performance"?

Nominative statements, reflecting propositions about "I am," are important to define clearly. For example, the idea that "I am a failure" may be analyzed for the meaning of "I am." "By 'I am' do you mean every behavior that you engage in is a failure? Is there something internal about you that is a failure? What is it and how would we know if someone else had that internal quality? By 'I am' do you mean stable and completely unchangeable across situations, so that you are a failure in every situation? Were you always a failure?"

As the patient examines the definitional unclarity inherent in her assumptions, she may be urged to reword the assumption or modify the definition. For example, "success" may be changed from "superior performance" to "behaviors that lead to obtaining goals." The therapist will find it useful to have the patient modify definitions to reflect a more behavioral content; rather than emphasize global traits (e.g., successful person), the definition might be rephrased as "specific behaviors in specific situations." For example, the dichotomous construct "success vs. failure as a person" then becomes specific behaviors that lead to obtaining some goals in some situations. The value in moving toward more behavioral definitions is that the patient will be able to see that specific behaviors are variable and modifiable, thus further challenging the patient's global negative labeling and hopelessness.

4. Internal Inconsistencies and Logical Errors

Maladaptive assumptions often contain logical inconsistencies. For example, the assumption that "I am a failure because I am single" is logically inconsistent. Consider the following interaction:

Therapist: You say that you are a failure if you are single. Would you agree that everyone who is married was once single?
Patient: Yes.
Therapist: Then does it follow from your definition that everyone who is married was once a failure?

Logical inconsistencies usually follow from labeling, all-or-nothing statements, and should statements. Each of these has an over-generalizing component such as:

1. I failed the test.
2. Therefore, I am a failure.

or

1. Bill rejected me at the party.
2. Therefore, everyone will reject me.

The first set of propositions implies that if you fail a test, you are a failure. But consider the following:

1. I did well on the test.
2. Therefore, I am a success.

or

1. Tom liked me at the party.
2. Therefore, everyone will like me.

This overgeneralization and labeling can be tested by asking what is implied if you succeed on the test. "Are you, then, a success? If you succeeded on a test in the past, but failed this test, how can you label yourself both a failure and a success? Isn't it more accurate to say, 'Sometimes I do better than I do at other times?'" Other logical inconsistencies may be illustrated, showing that the patient tends to overinclude negatives and underinclude positives.

Patients' self-labels are often a source of internal inconsistencies. For example, the perfectionistic patient who believes that he should be perfect or special may respond that he is worthless and a failure if he does not achieve perfection. The therapist may ask how he can reconcile the beliefs that he should be perfect and special if he believes that he is really worthless and a failure.

Another common logical error is to conclude that "I should" do something because "I desire it" or "others expect it of me." As a consequence, preferences become imperatives and concern about others' opinions becomes a source of obligation. The patient may be asked to distinguish between "I prefer success on this task" and "I should do well on this task." Similarly, the therapist can distinguish between "I like it when people like me" and "I should win their approval."

5. Double Standard Technique

The double standard technique is used to challenge the patient's willingness to apply her assumption to other people. For example, the assumption that "I am worthless if I am single" is challenged by asking the patient to list friends and colleagues who are single and their positive and negative qualities. Would the patient label these people as "worthless" because they are single?

Similarly, perfectionism is challenged by asking if the patient knows anyone who has ever made a mistake and therefore qualifies as imperfect. Would the patient label him as worthless?

The patient's unwillingness to generalize the assumption to other people is then examined. Is there some reason that one standard should apply to the patient and not to others? If so, what is the assumption that justifies the double standard? Patients who hold to perfectionism often believe that they are special or unique individuals for whom higher standards are applicable. This new underlying assumption of uniqueness is then examined.

6. Act in Opposition to the Assumption

The patient who holds the assumption that it would be "terrible if I were rejected" may be asked to collect information about that assumption by carrying out a behavioral experiment. For example, the patient is asked, "What specifically will happen that is so terrible if someone rejects you?" The patient may list a set of feelings ("I'll feel sad, depressed, awful"), or predictions about how others will respond ("Others will reject me").

These predictions may be tested by a behavioral experiment in which the patient seeks out or collects rejections. For example, the patient may be asked to approach opposite sex strangers and ask them out for a date. Similarly, if the patient's assumptions are based on perfectionism, he is asked to perform a number of tasks imperfectly and then see what happens. Does he become worthless or rejected by everyone? Or does nothing significantly negative occur?

7. Replacing Maladaptive Assumptions with Practical Assumptions

Although the patient may recognize the illogical or unrealistic nature of her assumption, she may be reluctant to abandon the assumption without a tenable alternative. We refer to this as a paradigmatic shift. Is the patient able to shift from a maladaptive to an adaptive assumption?

Maladaptive assumptions are rigid, demanding, moralistic, and almost impossible to live up to, since it is impossible to be perfect all the time or avoid rejection. The implications of these maladaptive assumptions are that the self becomes less worthy or that terrible things will happen.

We recommend replacing these assumptions with pragmatic-adaptive assumptions that involve qualifiers. For example, "It would be useful to do a good job most of the time, but it is not disastrous to be imperfect" is pragmatic because it is realistic, adaptive because it still motivates the individual, and it is qualified by "most of the time." Moreover, the pragmatic assumption deescalates negativity, for if the patient follows that assumption, nothing terrible will likely follow. In contrast, the maladaptive assumption contributes to anxiety and depression because it places unrealistic demands on the self or others (see Table 6–3).

8. Examining Evidence

Assumptions are not only proscriptive or prescriptive statements but are also propositions about reality. Consequently, they are open to possible disconfirmation. After the patient's assumptions have been identified and the terms defined, she is ready to evaluate the evidence for and against the assumption.

Table 6–3. Maladaptive vs. Pragmatic Assumptions

Maladaptive	Pragmatic
I must always be successful.	It's rewarding to be successful. I can learn from my mistakes.
If I'm not perfect, I'm a failure.	Everyone makes mistakes. If I make mistakes, then I'm human.
I need the approval of everyone.	It's rewarding to get approval. No one is liked by everyone. Even if someone disapproves of me, I can still do many rewarding things.
I need to be certain before I try something.	If I take risks, I may win some and lose some. I may be competent to handle surprises.
My partner should know what I want without my telling him.	People are not mind readers. It is my responsibility to tell my partner what my needs are.

The assumption "It is terrible if I am inferior," may be examined by listing all the negative and all the positive or neutral things that can happen if "I am inferior." The patient will discover that the only terrible thing that occurs when one is inferior is self-criticism, if she chooses to self-criticize. However, even if she is inferior to someone else she can still do all the things she did before.

The patient is asked to make a double-column listing of all the evidence supporting and all the evidence challenging the assumption. It is useful to ask the patient about the quality of evidence. The evidence that "I am a failure if I don't succeed at something" might be "I feel like a failure." The patient might be asked if this emotional reasoning would be considered good quality evidence of failure or guilt by a court.

In weighing the evidence it is useful to have the patient go through and comment on each point of evidence. This helps him reflect further on the quality and relevance of the evidence. He is then asked to balance 100 points between the evidence for and against the assumption.

A contrasting but pragmatic assumption may then be offered. The patient is asked to offer evidence for and against this assumption and evaluate the quality and balance of that evidence. The resultant balance of the maladaptive assumption is then compared with the balance of the pragmatic assumption, and the patient is asked, "Which assumption is the most convincing assumption to you, given the evidence?" The patient is further queried as to which evidence seems to be the most compelling.

9. Externalization of Voices

After the patient has gone through these steps, the therapist may use externalization of voices to test the patient's continuing belief in the assumption. Patient and therapist reverse the roles of the negative assumption or rational response. The therapist may use this technique to diagnose the extent to which the patient may need further help challenging the assumption.

Therapist: If you failed at that exam, it means you're a failure.
Patient: What do you mean by a "failure"?
Therapist: A failure is someone who can't do anything right.
Patient: Well, it's clear then that I'm not a failure. There are lots of things that I do right. I'm doing pretty well at work, I have friends, I'm doing OK in other courses.
Therapist: Well, those things don't count. Anyone can do them.
Patient: Just because others can do what I do doesn't mean I'm a failure.
Therapist: Everyone does better than you.
Patient: That's not true. I'm certainly above average in some things. I don't have to do everything well in order to do lots of other things well.
Therapist: If you fail that exam, then you won't be able to do anything.
Patient: No, that's not true either. I can still do all the things I've always done even if I did fail that exam.
Therapist: You seemed to handle these thoughts quite well. Are there any thoughts that were especially difficult for you to handle?

If the patient has had difficulty playing the role of the rational response in the externalization of voices for certain automatic thoughts, then the therapist may reverse roles and take the role of the rational response.

10. Feared Fantasy

One form of externalization of voices is the feared fantasy technique. In this technique the therapist identifies the patient's underlying feared situation and engages in role play with the patient as to how to handle the feared situation. For example, one patient feared that twenty years after graduating from college he would meet his peers at a college reunion and be ridiculed for not being as successful as they were. The therapist plays the role of the obnoxious classmate acting in a condescending and insulting manner toward the patient. The patient then gives the rational response, refuting and challenging the negative statements of the classmate.

Therapist (playing role of obnoxious classmate): Oh, I see, Bill, that you aren't as successful as I am. That must really bother you.
Patient: Not really. My self-esteem doesn't depend on how much money I make.
Classmate: Well, it should. Everything else you do is worthless.
Patient: No, it's not worthless. I have a good relationship with my wife and kids. And my work is rewarding.
Classmate: How can your work be rewarding if you're not making lots of money?
Patient: There are lots of rewarding things that I do. There's the challenge of my work, my colleagues, the satisfaction that I have integrity.
Classmate: Well, I can't respect you.
Patient: That's more your problem than it is mine.

Other feared-fantasy role plays involving imagery and cognitive rehearsal allow the patient to confront his worst (and probably least likely to occur) fears and see that he might be able to cope with them. This decreases the patient's anxiety about his current problems.

Many of the techniques that are used in evaluating automatic thoughts are also useful in evaluating assumptions. Assumptions are more pervasive—they lie dormant but always available to the individual, to make him more vulnerable to depression and anxiety. One can argue that automatic thoughts are state-dependent, in that when one is depressed or anxious the automatic thought is there. In contrast, underlying assumptions are part of the patient's general belief system and may continue to operate even when the patient is not symptomatic. Thus, it is not enough to challenge the automatic thought—"I will be rejected"—it is even more important to challenge the assumption "I need acceptance from everyone to value myself."

At a deeper, even more general level than the automatic thought are the personal schemas that bias the individual toward particular content areas.

TESTING SCHEMAS

Beck's cognitive model is based on the view that stressful life events may activate an individual's underlying schemas or predispositions. For some, divorce may activate concerns about abandonment ("I'll be deserted by people"); helplessness ("I can't take care of myself"); lack of control ("I couldn't keep my wife; how can I control anything?"), or unlovability ("I must be flawed—unlovable—because of this"). Beck and Freeman (1990) have proposed that personality disorders may be characterized by differences in schematic content: for example, paranoid (betrayal), compulsive (control, imperfection), dependent (abandonment), avoidant (rejection), narcissistic (uniqueness) or histrionic (attractiveness) personality disorders.

The meaning of an event will depend on the individual's typical schema. Information will be selectively attended to and recalled in relationship to the schema. The dependent individual will watch for any signs of abandonment or rejection and will selectively recall information regarding past abandonment.

Relationship between Schemas, Assumptions, and Automatic Thoughts

Beck (1976), Beck and colleagues (1979), Leahy and Beck (1988) have viewed schemas as central to pathology, leading to automatic thoughts and maladaptive assumptions which, in turn, maintain the schema. For example, the dependent individual (with the schema of abandonment) will have a set of assumptions regarding abandonment:

"I must be pleasing to others or they will leave me."
"If someone isn't always focused on reassuring me, then they will leave me."
"If I assert myself, then I'll be rejected."
"Any relationship is better than no relationship."
"I can't take care of myself; I can't make myself happy."

As a result of these assumptions, the dependent individual is selectively focused on any evidence of abandonment. Consider the following automatic thought distortions.

Mind reading: He doesn't like me.
Personalizing: She must be in a bad mood because of something I said.
Fortune telling: I'll be left alone.
All-or-nothing thinking: Without her, I have nothing.
Labeling: I'm nothing without a partner.

As these examples illustrate, schemas are maintained by distortions in assumptions and automatic thoughts. Modifying the automatic thought or the assumption may not alter the individual's vulnerability if the schema remains intact.

Compensation and Avoidance of Schemas

Bowlby (1980) and Beck and Freeman (1990) have proposed that individuals attempt to adapt to their schematic vulnerability. Similar arguments are made by Guidanno and Liotti (1983), Leahy (1985, 1991, 1995), and Young (1990). Using the example of dependency, the individual who fears abandonment may compensate for this vulnerability by being extremely pleasing, nonassertive, or even seductive. He or she may believe that if one is perfectly pleasing, abandonment can be avoided. Another adaptation is to avoid risk of abandonment. For example, the individual may avoid getting involved with people or sabotage a relationship so as to have control over the abandonment. (Theodore Reik referred to this as "victory over defeat.")

The individual who believes that he is basically stupid and lazy may compensate by making compulsive demands on himself to perform perfectly. Or in contrast, he may avoid any challenge and seek a life of least resistance so as not to risk engaging in effort and discovering that his schema is true.

Because individuals may be compensating for and avoiding their schematic content, it is possible they have never directly challenged their underlying schemas. We have found many patients are surprised to learn that they view significant events through the lens of a single schema and are even more surprised that their spouse has a different schema. For example, the husband's schema may be one of being in control (or not controlled) whereas the wife's schema may be one of being misunderstood and ignored. Consequently, when the wife ventilates her feelings, hoping for understanding and a closer relationship, the husband interprets this as a violation of his boundaries and demands greater distance. Schema conflict is a frequent source of problems in marriages.

Identifying Schemas

We find that the vertical-descent procedure ("What if that's true? What would that mean to you?") often leads one to the underlying schema. With the dependent personality, the vertical descent may lead to the following answers:

"If he's angry, he won't want to stay —> He'll leave me.—> I'll be alone —> I won't be able to take care of myself—> I can't make myself happy by myself."

This illustrates that conflict for this individual results in abandonment and helplessness. Contrast this with an individual with a positive schema:

"If he's angry, it doesn't mean anything. People have conflicts."
[What if he left?]—>
"I'd be unhappy for a while, but I have lots of friends and my work is interesting" —>
"I can take care of myself."

Another way of identifying schemas is to examine the pattern of current conflicts for the patient. Does the patient get unusually upset over issues related to abandonment, rejection, control, or loss of unique status? A narcissistic patient would often become angry over what he perceived as humiliation. With the therapist, colleagues, his girlfriend, and even with the policy of having to pay for therapy, he saw many things in terms of humiliation.

Developmental Analysis

Cognitive therapists are not limited to the here and now. Similar to the psychodynamic therapist, the cognitive therapist will examine the origins of current schemas in the patient's childhood (Beck and Freeman 1990, Leahy 1985, 1991, 1995,

Young 1990). The therapist may simply point out the pattern of schemas and ask, "How did you learn to think that way? Who told you that?" For example, a successful doctor had a series of unsatisfactory extramarital affairs, even though he viewed his wife as vastly more desirable than these other women. The therapist pointed out that his affairs seemed to suggest two issues—hostility toward women and an attempt to make sure that someone was there in case his marriage failed. Developmental analysis resulted in his recognition that he never forgave his mother for leaving his father (when the patient was 8) and that he had his first panic attack the day before he got married. His automatic thought before the wedding was, "What if she leaves me?" Consequently, he began a series of "hedging" relationships with other women.

Developmental analysis is also able to point out to the patient how he has been maintaining his schema for many years, either through compensations or avoidance. A successful executive, driven by perfectionist self-demands, recognized that despite his many successes he had never really challenged his mother's message, "You are not that smart." Using developmental analysis, the therapist engaged the patient in an "empty-chair" challenge in which the patient had to tell his mother why she was wrong. This resulted in considerable relief of his self-criticism.

Submitting Schemas to Cognitive Disputation

Self-schemas may be tested using all of the techniques mentioned in previous sections on automatic thoughts and assumptions. The schema, "I am helpless without a man," may be tested and examined using the following techniques:

What is the cost and benefit of believing you are helpless without a man?

How would you define helpless?
What is the evidence for and against the idea that you are
     helpless?
Are you ever able to accomplish anything?
Do you believe that other women are helpless without a man?
What is your reason for applying one standard to yourself and
     another to others?
What are some things that you can do today and this week to
     challenge the idea that you are helpless?
Would you be willing to schedule some behaviors that contra-
     dict the idea that you are helpless?
What are the advantages of being able to do things on your
     own?

Developing More Realistic Schemas

Paradigm shifts arise when one world view is replaced by what
is perceived as a better world view (Kuhn 1970). Similarly,
maladaptive schemas may be replaced by more realistic ones,
thereby giving the patient something more achievable (see
Table 6–4).

Table 6–4. Replacing Maladaptive with Adaptive Schemas

Maladaptive Schema	New Schema
Superior	Having a variety of positives, but able to appreciate the everyday and to learn from experience
Controlled	Willing to be flexible and cooperative and recognize that not everything is an issue of control
Helpless	Recognizing that I can't get everything I want, but I can reward myself
Abandoned	Recognizing that relationships are not always permanent, but that conflicts are part of life and I can take care of myself if I need to

One may argue that one finds safety at the "center of his fear." To overcome a fear of heights, one climbs mountains. Similarly, developing more realistic schemas may require practicing in opposition to the schema. The compulsive patient may be asked to practice making mistakes. In one case, a patient was asked to make mistakes intentionally on every check he wrote for that month. He expressed considerable relief on completing the assignment when he learned that no one really cared about these mistakes. In another case, a dependent woman who consistently dated problematic men was asked not to date any men for a month. This initially raised her anxiety, but as the assignment was carried forward she realized she was often much better off doing things on her own, and that her problems were often due to making poor choices out of desperation.

Anticipating Problems

We realize that life events often override the effective work that any therapist may perform. However, once we recognize the patient's schematic content, therapist and patient may anticipate the kinds of situations that will give rise to a typical pattern of automatic thoughts, assumptions, and schemas. We view this as the "inoculation phase" of therapy during which therapist and patient troubleshoot the vulnerabilities of the patient. The therapist may assist the patient in writing out a self-help program for these anticipated problems. The dependent patient, vulnerable to abandonment, may be instructed in a life plan of developing supportive social networks and productive work of her own. She and the therapist may anticipate her belief that she cannot function on her own. Consequently, the therapist may encourage her to plan independent activities, rely on an activity schedule, list examples of typical automatic thoughts and challenges to these thoughts, and plan to act in opposition to the schema. The patient should be told that this vulnerability may always be present, but she now has the tools to challenge negative thinking.

III

SPECIFIC APPLICATIONS

7

DEPRESSION

Cognitive therapy is best known as a treatment for depression (Beck et al. 1979). Initially developed as a treatment for reactive depressions uncomplicated by personality disorders or other dual diagnoses, the cognitive therapy model has since been utilized for a variety of depressive disorders including major depressive disorder, dysthymia, atypical depression, personality disorders associated with depression, and marital conflict contributing to depression. In this chapter, we will review the typical assessment tools utilized in evaluating depression from both a traditional and cognitive approach and the behavioral and cognitive techniques that can effectively be used with these patients.

EVALUATION

General symptom levels of depression, as evaluated by the BDI, SCL 90R, and the Hamilton are used as baseline measures to evaluate the efficacy of the treatment. For example, the patient who initially presents with a BDI score of 35 (severe depression), may evaluate how effective his therapy is by taking the BDI every week and examining changes in the depression score. This continued monitoring of scores is useful for depressed patients who tend to focus on what has not changed rather than on what has changed; the depressed patient whose BDI has decreased from 35 to 23 in six weeks may complain that he notices no progress because he is still depressed. The clinician may agree that the patient is still depressed, but point out that the depression is less. Moreover, because the BDI assesses specific symptom areas and levels of those symptoms, the clinician may also point out that the level of hopelessness, self-criticism and indecisiveness have changed.

Continual assessment on the BDI may also reveal that the depression has not changed, or that the depression level is unpredictable. This can also be useful in evaluating which specific techniques have not worked and indicating that new interventions—whether behavioral, cognitive, or pharmacological—may be needed. By sharing with the patient the continued evaluation of the depression, the clinician reinforces the patient's role as informed consumer, increasing her motivation to collaborate with the therapist.

Assessment also focuses on specific cognitive distortions and assumptions. We use the first three sessions for assessment of the patient's problems, focusing on family, occupational, interpersonal, and therapeutic history. The cognitive assessment seeks to evaluate what the patient is thinking when he or she is depressed or anxious.

Therapist: You said that your first episode of depression occurred right after the breakup with your boyfriend several years ago. Let's examine what you were thinking then that was making you depressed. "When we broke up, I felt depressed because I thought . . ."

Patient: I'll never be happy again.

Therapist: "I'll never be happy again because I think . . ."

Patient: No one will want me.

Therapist: "No one will want me because . . ."

Patient: I have nothing to offer.

This cognitive assessment during the intake reveals that the patient may be vulnerable to depression over interpersonal losses because she believes that relationships end because of her permanent, universally undesirable traits. For example, she may believe that she is uninteresting, unattractive, and unrewarding and that no one will ever want her. Furthermore, she may also believe that she cannot be happy without a man—an underlying assumption that should be examined with the help of the therapist.

The initial assessment of depression also includes evaluation of behavioral deficits and excesses as well as reinforcement possibilities. Behavioral deficits include the low frequency of behaviors that could reasonably lead to reinforcements. Is the patient generally nonassertive, unskilled in rewarding others, involved in asocial and passive behavior (e.g., constantly watching television), hypersomniac, and unskilled in communication and listening skills? Deficits may also include the tendency not to meet fundamental biological needs. For example, is the patient often sleep-deprived or does he fail to maintain adequate nutrition and hygiene? These deficits may dramatically augment any vulnerability to depression, anxiety, and anger.

Behavioral excesses include a high frequency of dysfunctional behaviors such as complaining, performing monotonous tasks, engaging in hostile or nonrewarding behavior with others, ignoring others, or engaging in self-abusive behavior.

Does the patient fail to engage in self-reward following the completion of positive behaviors? Many depressed patients may obtain considerable achievement, but fail either to notice their achievements or reward themselves for these achievements; they are deficient in self-praise. Finally, is the patient spending considerable time in nonrewarding environments? Many depressed patients may spend significant time with people who do not reward them or who may even punish them. A detailed behavioral evaluation should include the marital or significant relationships in the patient's life.

SOCIALIZING THE PATIENT TO THERAPY

Cognitive therapy is a collaborative approach whereby the patient and therapist work together to evaluate and modify problem areas. After the initial assessment has been completed, and the patient has finished the required self-evaluation forms (e.g., the BDI, BAI, SCL 90R, SCID II, Locke-Wallace and any other forms deemed relevant), therapist and patient meet for an overview of the presenting problems.

Therapist: I would like to review the forms and the interviews we have conducted thus far so we can both understand the problems we will be dealing with. These self-report forms assess depression, anxiety, phobias, anger, interpersonal problems, and your self-concept. In addition, we have also assessed your level of satisfaction in your marriage. This form (Beck Depression Inventory) indicates you have a relatively high level of depression—a score of 25—the higher the score, the more depression. We would hope to reduce this score to below 10. Your depression seems to be focused on self-critical thinking, indecisiveness, and feelings of hopelessness. This other form (the SCL 90R) assesses 90 different psychiatric symptoms, indicating that along with the depression I mentioned, you also have significant anxiety and some obsessive symptoms, such as worrying a lot. This other form (SCID II) indicates some interpersonal and self issues, focused on avoidance of others because of your concern about rejection and concern about everything having to be just right (compulsive personality). We can also see that your relationship with your wife is troubling you. On the Locke-Wallace form, we find that scores below 100 are problematic. As you can see, your score is 75, somewhat below the standard. We might want to examine how we can improve the marital situation in order to lessen your depression. Quite often, depression results from marital problems, so it might be worth trying to improve that relationship.

In your therapy, we can address how to increase your ability to experience pleasure, how to examine and modify some of your thinking, and how to improve your relationships. We focus mostly on the here and now, rather than examining the details of your childhood relationships. As your therapist, I will be active; there are times I will challenge your thinking or suggest some ways of changing things. You may tape-record sessions and keep the tapes for your own review—this will reinforce what we do. Part of your therapy is self-help, which includes homework exercises that you can use to generalize or practice what you learn in sessions. I will ask you for feedback on what we are doing, both negative and positive. You can also ask me for feedback, why we're doing what we're doing in sessions or to clarify something.

During our first few interviews, I often asked you what you were thinking when you felt sad or anxious. Those thoughts are called automatic thoughts because they occur automatically or spontaneously. You indicated a number of thoughts that caused you to feel upset, such as mind-reading ("He thinks I'm a loser"), fortune telling ("I'll never be happy") and labeling ("I'm a failure"). You also seem to have assumptions or rules that make you more vulnerable, such as your demanding thoughts that you have to be perfect or your thought that you must be sure that people like you.

Does this describe how you think and feel?

The therapist will punctuate the feedback presented with questions such as, "Does this seem like how you feel?" She can then move on to present a diagnosis.

Therapist: My impression is that you are now experiencing a significant level of depression and that you have had two other depressive episodes in the past. When you're depressed you seem to become overly self-critical, indecisive, and you reduce your level of activity. In addition, your depression is now associated with marital problems.

There are four causes of depression we can address in your treatment. These include your behavior, your thoughts, your marital or interpersonal relations, and your biochemistry. You should understand that there are a number of medications that have a high probability of reducing your depression. If you choose to use them, you may or may not also choose cognitive therapy. All the final choices are up to you.

Some therapists may think that the use of such an extensive intake might alienate patients. Certainly there are some who refuse to fill out forms; often these are narcissistic, paranoid, and histrionic patients who may need some supportive work with the therapist before the intake proceeds. However, we have found that patients appreciate the structured and diligent manner in which information is collected, and they express a strong interest in the idea of an active, self-help approach. We attempt to reinforce the cognitive therapy approach by requiring either one of David Burns's excellent self-help books,

Feeling Good: The New Mood Therapy (1980) or *The Feeling Good Handbook* (1989). Other appropriate self-help books can be assigned to patients with specific problems, such as Edna Foa and Reid Wilson's *Stop Obsessing* (1991).

INITIAL SESSIONS: ACTIVITY SCHEDULING AND ELICITING AUTOMATIC THOUGHTS

The first homework assignment is often the first two or three chapters in either of Burns's books. In addition, the patient is asked to fill out an activity schedule for the week. As with all homework assignments, the therapist offers a rationale for the assignment. The rationale for the activity schedule is the following:

Therapist: It is important that we both know how you spend your time and how your moods fluctuate with what you do. I am going to ask you to keep track of your pleasure and mastery (that is, your sense of competence) for each hour of the next week. This will tell us how your feelings vary with what you do. We can use this later to help you decide if you would like to assign yourself new activities for the following week. (The therapist then shows the patient how to fill out the activity schedule.)

The following session is then focused on reviewing the activity schedule, assigning rewarding behaviors, and decreasing negative behaviors. Demonstrating that moods vary with behaviors helps the patient realize that his moods are potentially under his control.

Tracking mood variation is also important in recording

automatic thoughts. The patient is told that an automatic thought is a thought that comes spontaneously, is associated with a negative mood, and seems highly plausible. Automatic thoughts are either true or false. The therapist does not challenge automatic thoughts; rather, he assists the patient in examining these thoughts. During the session, the therapist asks the patient what he's thinking when he feels upset.

Therapist: When you think of going to the party, you say you feel anxious. Try to complete the sentence: "As I walk into the party, I feel anxious because I think . . ."
Patient: I'll be rejected. No one will like me.
Therapist: OK. These are examples of automatic thoughts. During the next week, I'd like you to write down two automatic thoughts each day. Use this form—your emotion in the left column, your thought in the right column (see Table 7–1).

TESTING AND MODIFYING THOUGHTS

1. Identifying Automatic Thoughts

Once the patient has recorded thoughts that are associated with negative moods, the therapist must distinguish automatic

Table 7–1. Thought and Mood Monitoring

Mood	Thought
Anxious	I'll be rejected.
Sad	No one likes me.
Hopeless	I'll always be alone.

thoughts from feelings and rhetorical questions. Automatic thoughts are defined as statements about reality potentially open to disconfirmation, such as "I'm a failure," "He doesn't like me," or "It's awful." In contrast, feelings are reports of emotions or sensations that are always veridical, such as "I feel lonely, sad, angry, anxious."

The patient must be instructed in the A–B–C Paradigm—that is, antecedent (situation), belief (automatic thought), and consequence (the emotion or behavior). For example, A–"I was fired" (antecedent situation) —> B–"I think I have nothing to look forward to" (belief) —> therefore, C–"I feel sad and hopeless" (consequent emotions). As inspection of Table 7–2 indicates, the same situation can give rise to a variety of different beliefs and feelings. The therapist should not conclude that she knows what the patient's interpretation is; in fact, some of the most important insights that patient and therapist gain are through examining the patient's idiosyncratic interpretation of events.

The distinction between thought and feeling is important because we can question the evidence and logic of "I have nothing to look forward to," but we cannot question the fact or emotion, "I feel sad." Similarly, the patient must learn to distinguish rhetorical questions, such as, "Why am I always failing?" or "Why does this happen to me?", from automatic

Table 7–2. A–B–C Technique

Antecedent	Belief	Consequence
Lost job	I have nothing to look forward to.	Hopeless, sad
Lost job	I'm a failure.	Sad
Lost job	My wife will reject me.	Anxious
Taking exam	I need an A.	Anxious
Insulted by colleague	He's awful.	Angry
Insulted by colleague	I must deserve this.	Sad

thoughts such as, "I am always failing" or "This is terrible." Rhetorical questions are not statements about reality (propositions) that are open to disconfirmation. To assist in this distinction the therapist may follow the rhetorical question with, "Are you saying, 'I'm always failing' "? Similarly, "What if?" rhetorical questions need to be translated into predictions. "What if I fail?" may, on inquiry, become "I'll fail" or "It would be terrible if I failed."

2. Rating Degree of Emotion and Degree of Belief

Having identified the emotion and the automatic thought, the patient must now quantify them. We use a scale between 0 percent and 100 percent. For sadness, 0 percent corresponds to the absence of any sadness, whereas 100 percent corresponds to "the greatest sadness imaginable." For anxiety, 0 percent corresponds to the absence of any anxious feelings, whereas 100 percent corresponds to panic. Middle points are identified in terms of qualifiers—e.g., slightly, somewhat, moderately, and very.

For degree of belief in the automatic thought, the patient rates the automatic thought between 0 percent (no belief) and 100 percent (absolute certainty), with middle points reflecting the same qualifiers.

3. Identifying Cognitive Distortions

Once the patient's automatic thoughts have been identified, recorded, and rated, he will then categorize them as cognitive distortions. It is important to point out to the patient that this does not mean that automatic thoughts are false; for example, the thought "He doesn't like me," which is categorized as mind reading, could be true. However, by categorizing them as distortions the patient may be assisted in finding patterns in his thinking—a pattern of mind reading, fortune telling or catastrophizing.

The patient is given a list of definitions of cognitive distortions from the Burns *Feeling Good Handbook*. Since the patient already has a list of automatic thoughts, he is asked to apply categories to each thought. A single automatic thought may fall into more than one category. The thought "She'll reject me" is both fortune telling and mind reading.

4. Defining Terms: Semantic Analysis

A powerful but simple intervention is to have the patient define the terms of the automatic thought. The therapist may introduce this by saying, "Before we can test out your thought, we have to know what the thought means; we have to define the terms you're using. Let's take your thought, 'I am a failure.' How would we define failure?" The patient may say that a "failure is someone who does not accomplish his goals." Once the patient has defined one pole of his construct, we then define the opposite pole: "How do you define success?" The patient might say that "success is attaining your goals." The therapist can go further and have the patient define "I am": does "I am" mean every behavior of the self or does it mean only a few behaviors? In challenging distortions of labeling, the definition of "I am" is important, since it is to the patient's benefit that he or she learn to focus on specific behaviors that fail rather than a self that fails.

A similar line of inquiry can be directed toward defining "rejection" or "awful" or "I can't stand it." With "I can't stand it" (which is catastrophic thinking), the patient is asked to define "I can't stand it." Does it mean "extremely unpleasant," "fatal," "something I don't want," or "the absence of all rewarding experiences"? How would we define "I can stand it"?:

Could we say that "you live through the experience" or "you still carry out other behaviors" or "you can tolerate and experience discomfort"?

5. Examining Evidence

The automatic thoughts that are the most disturbing, as defined by the degree of emotion associated with them, are selected first for examination. The patient is told that we will examine the evidence in favor of and against the automatic thought. The patient draws a line down the center of a page, writes the automatic thought at the top, and begins to list the evidence in each column (see Table 7–3).

For example, the automatic thought "I'm a failure," where failure has been defined by the absence of success, is tested by the patient reviewing any evidence in the present or past for or against this thought.

The patient may be asked to rate the quality of the evidence for each statement in the columns. For example, "If you had to present this as evidence to a jury to prove that you are a failure, how good would that evidence be?" Specifically,

Table 7–3. Testing the Thought "I'm a Failure"

For	Against
I didn't do as well as Bill on the job.	There are a number of tasks on the job that I do well.
	People have given me good feedback in the past.
I'm not married.	I graduated from college.
	I have a number of friends.
	I support myself.
I feel like a failure.	

"What would a jury think about the evidence 'I feel like a failure' "?

She is then asked to weigh the evidence for and against the proposition "I am a failure." The therapist says, "You have to divide 100 points between the evidence for and against. Does the evidence seem to support or not support the idea that you are a failure? How would you divide up the 100 points?" Patients are cautioned against simply counting the number of statements in each column. In the example given, the patient might say the evidence is 30 percent in favor and 70 percent against. The therapist asks, "So the evidence seems to go against the idea that you are a failure. What seems to be the strongest evidence that you are not a failure? What evidence indicates that you have some successes?"

The patient is then asked to rephrase "I am a failure" into a more realistic and less extreme statement. She might say, "I guess I have some successes and some failures." The therapist might ask if this statement has fewer negative connotations than "I am a failure." "If you succeed and fail at different things, what does this imply about your future behavior?"

6. Cost–Benefit Analysis

This technique is focused on the consequences of the automatic thought. The thought "I am a failure" is examined for the costs and benefits of holding this thought. The patient might say that the costs are that she will feel self-critical, sad, depressed, hopeless, and helpless; she may have a hard time seeing any benefits. In some cases self-critical patients believe that labeling themselves as failures will motivate them to try harder. This supposed benefit will be further examined when we deal with challenging underlying assumptions.

The therapist may ask the patient to imagine the costs–benefits if he no longer believed the thought as much. If the patient no longer believed that he was a failure, there might be no costs and the benefits would entail feeling better about the self, being more willing to take risks, and feeling more hopeful about the future.

7. Examining Logical Errors

The patient may be correct about the facts, but the conclusions drawn may be extreme and unjustified. "I did poorly on the exam" may turn out to be a fact, but the patient then concludes, "Therefore, I'm a failure" or "I'll be rejected by other people." These arbitrary inferences often have an all-or-nothing quality—"If I am rejected by one person, then I'm unlovable." The patient may be asked to construct an alternative conclusion; for example, "I didn't do well on this one task."

8. Alternative Explanations

Whether we call these "rational responses" or "alternative explanations," the purpose of this intervention is to provide the patient with a less negative perspective of the situation. The patient who labels herself a failure because a colleague performed better than she did might be asked, "Rather than label yourself as a failure, is there another way of looking at these events that is not as negative?" Possible alternatives might be logical disputations, such as "Just because she did better on this exam, it does not follow that I am a failure." Or the patient might look for alternative successes: "We both succeed at different things" or "I have several tasks on the job that I do well."

The patient who is "rejection sensitive" and encounters someone who does not encourage his advances might challenge the automatic thought "She can't stand me because I'm a loser" by saying "There are other people who like me," "I don't need everyone's approval," "She might be involved with someone else," "I might not be to her taste, but others could like me."

The patient can be encouraged to either generate or imitate alternative explanations through the use of role playing. The therapist can alternate with the patient, sometimes playing the role of the automatic thought and at other times the role of rational response. The patient is asked to indicate which automatic thoughts in the role play are not sufficiently challenged by the rational responses. These are then further examined through semantic techniques, costs–benefits, evidence, and role plays. Particularly common and/or troublesome automatic thoughts may be listed on flash cards, along with useful and effective rational responses, and given to the patient to repeat daily as cognitive rehearsal, and to be used whenever the automatic thought is activated. The patient is asked to indicate in each session which automatic thoughts became more (or less) powerful and which rational responses work or do not work.

9. Using the Daily Record of Dysfunctional Thoughts

The Daily Record of Dysfunctional Thoughts (DRDT) is used with all patients in cognitive therapy to assist them in identifying automatic thoughts, emotions, and rational responses. (See Figure 7–1.) The patient describes a situation associated with negative feelings. For example, a 32-year-old man who has been married for one year reports, "I had an argument with my wife and I yelled at her." He then indicates the emotions or feelings associated with the situation and the degree of emotion: "Sad (80 percent), Hopeless (60 percent), Self-critical (85 percent)." His automatic thoughts were, "I'm

Figure 7–1. DAILY RECORD OF DYSFUNCTIONAL THOUGHT

Situation	Emotion	Automatic Thought	Rational Response	Outcome
Describe the event and your train of thought at the time. What was going on when you became upset or bothered?	Identify and rate your emotions (0-100) Examples: sad, anxious, hopeless, angry, self-critical, frustrated.	"I felt...because I thought..." Rate your degree of belief in each thought (1-100%) Indicate which distortion you used*	How would you test or challenge this thought? Examine the costs/benefits, evidence, solutions, double standard. What advice would you give a friend with this problem? Argue back at the thought, put it in perspective.	How do you feel after you have challenged your thought? Rerate your emotions and automatic thoughts (0-100).

*Distortions: Mind reading, fortune telling, all-or-nothing thinking, labeling, discounting positives, catastrophizing, personalizing, unfair comparisions, unconfirmability, shoulds (musts), overgeneralizing, negative filter, emotional reasoning, perfectionistic.

abusive" (80 percent), "My marriage will fail" (75 percent), "I'm a failure" (80 percent). The therapist asks him to describe the situation leading up to the argument with his wife. She had been away for a week to get some furniture from a relative's home in another city. He told her on the phone that he had a

lot of bad memories associated with that place. She said he
didn't sound happy to hear from her, and he replied that he felt
upset about not seeing her, mentioning the bad memories
from the past. She then criticized him as "insecure, hostile, and
abusive." Rather than responding in kind, he said he was angry
and that her comments were unfair. They finished the conversation upset with each other. When we examined his evidence
for thinking he was abusive, he pointed to the fact that his wife
had so labeled him and revealed that he had been abused as a
child. His reasoning was: "people who were abused become
abusive."

He was able to come up with rational responses that effectively challenged his negative thoughts. "Getting angry is
normal, not abusive. I have never abused anyone. Just because I was abused as a kid doesn't mean that I will abuse
others." We also challenged the prediction that "My marriage
will fail." For example, "We love each other. We support each
other. Having disagreements and getting angry is a normal
part of marriage." He re-rated his beliefs in his automatic
thoughts, and he re-rated his emotions much more favorably
than before.

The therapist should be careful that the DRDT does not
simply become an exercise in positive thinking. Some may
believe that cognitive therapy is simply looking at the bright
side of things. To the contrary, cognitive therapy is looking at
both sides of a problem realistically. If problems are real, they
can be addressed by assisting the patient in modifying behavior and communication and changing the situation. Furthermore, the rational responses should be relevant to the
automatic thoughts; they should provide evidence, logic, and
arguments that contradict the negative thought. Simply saying, "Our marriage is good" is not as effective as noting, "We
love each other, we support each other, we enjoy doing things
together, and we communicate about how to make things
better." Therapist and patient should explore if they have
built a strong enough case against the negative thought.

Convincing logical and empirical arguments are far more effective than faint attempts to please the therapist with affirmations.

MODIFYING SPECIFIC SYMPTOMS OF DEPRESSION

A distinct advantage of the cognitive therapy approach is that it directly addresses specific symptoms. The most common symptoms of depression include self-criticism, hopelessness, indecisiveness, lack of pleasure, and insomnia. Sadness, of course, is a prime symptom of depression, but we view this as a consequence of other symptoms. We will describe specific interventions for each of these symptoms.

1. Self-criticism: "I'm a failure."

How much do you believe this, from 0 percent to 100 percent? How would you define "failure?" How would you define "success?" What is a successful behavior? Are there different degrees of success? Have you had any partial successes in anything? Have you ever accomplished a goal? What is the evidence for and against the thought, "I have had some successes?" Are you focusing only on what you did not succeed at and discounting what you have succeeded at? What is the consequence of this thinking? Would you label someone else a failure given the same information?

2. Hopelessness: "I'll always be depressed. I'll never find anyone."

What specific behavior or thought or situation do you think will never change? Are you saying that it can never improve? Have you had hopeless thoughts in the past? Have some of them not come true? Are your negative moods always permanent or sometimes temporary? Do they fluctuate? Are there any times during the week that your mood is even slightly better? Is that positive change associated with anything particular? What is your reason for believing that (a particular thought, behavior, or situation) can never change? Have any of your previous thoughts, behaviors, or situations changed? What are some short-term goals over the next week that you can accomplish? Do you have any long-term goals you could begin to plan?

Even if cognitive therapy does not work, have you exhausted every possible treatment for depression? Every medication? Every kind of psychotherapy—behavioral, interpersonal, psychodynamic, marital? What do you know about electroshock therapy? Do you often conclude that things are hopeless and give up, thereby confirming your negative thought that nothing can change? Are you willing to try an experimental attitude toward changing yourself; are you willing to try new ways of behaving or thinking to test whether they can be effective? Are you willing to count a small improvement as a worthwhile improvement?

3. *Indecisiveness*: "I can't decide what to say to my boss."

Specifically, what are the alternatives (decisions, actions) you are considering? List the costs and benefits for each alternative—now and in the future. What is your evidence that these are the costs and benefits? How sure are you of these consequences? If the negatives occurred, how would you cope? What is the benefit of making a decision and getting it out of the way? Are there any alternatives in addition to these alternatives? Are you willing to do things you don't want to do? Are you trying to assure certainty in an uncertain world?

4. *Lack of pleasure*: "I don't enjoy anything anymore."

Use the activity schedule and rate your pleasure and mastery for every hour of the week. Note specific behaviors that you engage in every hour. Is there any pattern to your pleasure ratings? Do they increase or decrease depending on what you're doing? List some activities you used to enjoy before you became depressed? Are you willing to assign some of these activities to yourself, in small amounts? What is the alternative to engaging in pleasurable behavior? Is that alternative more or less likely to help you make progress on your depression? What would you lose by engaging in pleasurable behavior? What do you stand to gain? Are you waiting to feel inspired to take action before you are willing to take action? Is it possible that the motivation or desire to do things may come after you have done them? Are you putting the cart before the horse? Do you have anti-pleasure thoughts, comparing how this activity feels now to how it felt before you got depressed? Is it reasonable to expect to feel as much pleasure when you are depressed as when you are not depressed? Are you willing to make an investment in engaging in activities for a period of time until the pleasure kicks in? If you were trying to get into shape and were going to a gym, would you expect to get into shape immediately? Are effects immediate or cumulative? When you engage in most behaviors, do you criticize yourself?

5. *Insomnia*: "I'm always exhausted. I can't sleep."

Over the next week, keep track of the time you go to bed, any time you get out of bed at night, and the time you wake up. Track any naps during the day. (This establishes our baseline measure.) The following week, schedule going to bed at the same time every night and getting up at the same time every morning, no matter how little sleep you've had. Do not take any naps. If possible, eliminate sedatives and stimulants (e.g., caffeine products). Limit or eliminate any fluid intake three hours before you go to bed. Use the bed only for sleep and sex; do not lie or sit in bed reading, talking on the phone, watching TV, listening to music, or ruminating. Do not engage in stimulating exercise, conversations, or any other activities that might make you anxious two hours before you go to bed. If you are lying in bed for twenty minutes and can't sleep, get up and go into another room and do something boring. If you have gotten out of bed because you are worried, write down your automatic thoughts and challenge them. Make a specific plan for behavior for the next day or week. Assign "worry time" for the next day, a time to focus on any worries. When you go back to bed, do not try to go to sleep. Avoid imperatives or self-commands, such as "I've got to get to sleep." Remember there is nothing catastrophic about losing some sleep. It is an inconvenience. Practice giving up or surrendering to the idea that you are lying there relaxing. Focus on relaxing, not sleeping.

SUMMARY

I see patients for an average number of twenty-eight sessions. This is a relatively short duration, compared with patients in psychodynamic therapy, but it actually may be a bit higher than the number of sessions for patients seen in cognitive therapy. Most outcome evaluation studies of cognitive therapy utilize a treatment format of about twenty sessions, with two sessions per week for the initial two or three weeks. It is useful to periodically review progress with the BDI administered every session for severely depressed patients. These reviews can help the patient and therapist determine the time at which phasing back therapy is plausible. (One rule might be, "Three weeks with a BDI below 10.")

We recommend phasing back rather than complete termination because it helps the patient use booster sessions over several months to reinforce the self-help components of the therapy. The patient is urged to continue using the Daily Record of Dysfunctional Thoughts and activity scheduling to prevent further depression.

In arranging for phasing out and eventual termination, it may be helpful to focus the patient on his specific pattern of depression (e.g., self-criticism, withdrawal, low activity level) and his specific assumptions or schemas that make him vulnerable. For example, patients who are vulnerable to social rejection should focus their attention on the assumptions that they need approval from everyone to feel worthwhile or that rejection is catastrophic. It is instructive to patients who have kept a written record of their automatic thoughts to review their past predictions and thoughts and to examine how fallacious they have been. We refer to this as the inoculation phase. "What would you do if you had that thought again? How would you handle rejection (failure, disappointment, etc.) in the future?" The goal in preparing the patient for phase-out and termination is for self-help to continue even when the patient is no longer symptomatic. The patient might object, "Do you mean that I have to challenge my negative thinking for the rest of my life?" The therapist can respond, "Do you need to exercise to keep in shape for the rest of your life?" Self-help is conceived as a life-long opportunity that empowers the patient to be his own therapist.

8

ANXIETY DISORDERS

In recent years there has been an increased awareness of the ubiquity of anxiety. In the national survey of *DSM-III-R* disorders in the non-clinical population, anxiety disorders accounted for the highest lifetime prevalence (25 percent) of all categories, with anxiety disorders proving to be of longer duration than affective disorders. Of all anxiety disorders, the most commonly diagnosed was social phobia. Furthermore, most individuals presenting with anxiety disorder also present with other diagnosable disorders—another anxiety disorder, depression, or substance abuse.

It is beyond the scope of this book to present a review of the relevant literature on anxiety disorders. Beck and colleagues' (1985) *Anxiety Disorders and Phobias* and Barlow's (1988) *Anxiety and Its Disorders* are excellent reviews of research, theory, and clinical application. However, this chapter reviews some general approaches to the treatment of anxiety disorders and focuses to a greater extent on the treatment of panic and obsessive-compulsive disorder.

PANIC DISORDER

In *DSM-IV*, patients may be diagnosed as having panic disorder with or without agoraphobia, and agoraphobia without panic. Furthermore, agoraphobia varies from mild to severe. Panic attacks are characterized by palpitations, sweating, trembling. shortness of breath, feelings of choking, chest pain, nausea, dizziness, derealization or depersonalization, fear of losing control or going crazy, fear of dying, paresthesia, and chills or hot flashes. Panic disorder is diagnosed if the patient has recurrent panic attacks followed by a month of worry over future panic or behavioral avoidance related to the fear of panic attacks. The importance of anticipatory anxiety is a clear part of the diagnosis of panic disorder.

The cognitive model of panic with agoraphobia places considerable emphasis on the patient's misinterpretations of anxiety. According to this model, the individual's initial panic attacks may be the result of genetic or biological vulnerabilities or increased stress. These initial, unexpected panic attacks are often interpreted by the patient as catastrophic: "I'm having a heart attack" or "I'm going crazy." As a result, the patient becomes sensitized and overly focused on internal signs of arousal or feelings of collapse. As he focuses on these interoceptive stimuli (physiological sensations), he may misinterpret normal sensations as dangerous: "My heart is pounding. Therefore, I'm having a heart attack" or "I'm feeling dizzy. Therefore, I will collapse." These misinterpretations result in increased sensations of arousal or collapse and the desire to escape. Agoraphobia develops as a result of avoidance conditioning as the individual learns to avoid many situations that he or she believes may lead to these feared sensations.

The key element in the cognitive model of panic is that the individual has a fear of panic attacks. Ironically, many patients presenting with agoraphobia may have very few panic attacks, precisely because they are avoiding the very situations that may arouse their anxiety. As a result, the clinician needs to evaluate the patient for situations that are avoided and the patient's interpretations of anxiety or panic. We have divided the treatment approach into five phases.

Evaluation. Panic disorder patients often present with agoraphobia—consequently, we shall focus on these individuals here. In the evaluation, the clinician should assess the history of panic attacks, situations that initially and subsequently gave rise to the panic, and the patient's attempts to cope with panic and the anticipation of panic. Many panickers self-medicate with alcohol or abuse Xanax and Valium. Panickers will attempt to cope with their fear of panic by having "safe people" to accompany them on short trips to the store or walks outdoors. Agoraphobics will often have supplies delivered home, avoid public transportation, and insist that others drive (lest they have a panic attack and lose control). They may report fears of crossing bridges, driving through tunnels, traveling in planes or trains, being in stairwells, elevators, and restaurants. In each case, the fear is not of the danger inherent in the place or situation, but rather that a panic attack will occur and escape will be blocked. Many panickers fear losing control and embarrassing themselves. Because of the curtailment of their activity and their tendency to hide their fears (thereby adding to their belief that they are all alone with their problem), many panickers report being depressed.

Socializing the patient. Educating the patient about the nature of panic and agoraphobia is an essential part of treatment. We indicate to panickers that many fears that comprise agoraphobia are innate and, in the early evolution of the species, were adaptive. For example, the fear of open spaces (and anxiety at viewing an unobscured horizon) is found in many species that are potential prey: if a mouse crosses an open field it is an easy target for attack by a cat or owl. Anxiety about being in closed spaces, being alone, on heights, bridges, and in tunnels may also reflect innate fears that were adaptive.

Stress reduction. Since general anxiety may make the patient more vulnerable to panic, each patient is assisted in general stress reduction. All patients are instructed in deep-muscle relaxation. (The reader is referred to Arnold Lazarus's (1977) excellent description of a progressive muscle-relaxation script.) Specific areas of stress are identified and the patient is assisted in identifying automatic thoughts and assumptions that add to stress. Anxious patients often engage in catastrophic fortune telling: ("I'll fail. I'll get fired"); negative filter ("Look at how poorly I did on that one item"); and personalizing ("I'm responsible for the whole thing"). Underlying assumptions of needing approval and perfectionism are also examined.

An important component of stress reduction for patients is their attitude toward anxiety. Many panickers have an all-or-nothing view of anxiety ("I have to get rid of all anxiety") or perfectionism about control ("I have to be in control of myself all the time"). Agoraphobic and social-phobic patients experience anxiety transparency ("People can see I'm anxious"), and they believe everyone would reject them if others knew how anxious they were. Cognitive therapy challenges those anxiety thoughts. The patient who fears that she will do poorly on a test may be asked the following questions:

"Specifically, how poorly do you think you'll do? What is the evidence that you will do well or poorly? If you did poorly, what would that mean to you? What would happen in your life as a result of this test? How will you feel about this a month from now? A year from now? In what other areas of your life have you had some successful experiences? What would you say to a friend who had these thoughts? Why do you have a higher standard for yourself than for others? How often have your negative predictions proved wrong?"

A patient may be assisted in handling frequently occurring anxiety thoughts by using flash cards on which he has written the automatic thought on one side and several rational responses on the other side. The patient may use the Daily Record of Dysfunctional Thoughts (see Figure 7–1), which allows the patient to identify eliciting situations, emotions, thoughts, rational responses, and outcome. It is useful for patients to periodically review these records to note patterns and effective rational responses, and to examine how many of their negative thoughts have failed to come true.

Patients suffering from anxiety and depression frequently worry or ruminate such that their anxious thoughts seem to pervade their entire day. These patients may be assigned worry time during which they are told to spend thirty minutes per day focusing intensely on their worries. This technique combines satiation (exposure) with stimulus control (in that worrying is restrained to the stimuli of a specific time and place). We do not recommend thought-stopping since this technique often leads to thought-rebounding or an increase in anxious ruminations (see Wegner 1989).

Exposure to response hierarchy. Therapist and patient collaborate in constructing a list of situations that the patient avoids, from least to most feared. It is important for the patient to indicate what he or she fears: Is it the fear of losing control, going insane, having a heart attack, collapsing, or being unable to reach a toilet? The therapist should inquire about the different degrees of fear when the patient is alone or with someone in these situations. (Most panickers are more afraid when alone, because they view a companion as someone who can help them escape or call for help.) The patient assigns

subjective units of distress (ratings of anxiety) that are anticipated or experienced in each of these situations.

As therapy progresses, the patient is encouraged to gradually expose herself to these situations. For example, a 42-
year-old agoraphobic woman with a ten-year history of fear of
bridges, constructed a hierarchy of bridges she feared crossing, indicating her degree of fear if she was accompanied by
her husband or alone. Prior to crossing each bridge in her car,
she noted her prediction, (e.g., "I'll lose control and crash"),
her degree of belief in the prediction, and her anxiety level.
Each time she crossed the bridge she was required to record
the outcome methodically. ("What happened? Did your prediction prove false? What is your current anxiety level?") She was
asked to go back and forth over the same bridge until her
anticipatory anxiety had been reduced by half. Over the
course of a few weeks, she was crossing the longest bridges in
the Philadelphia area and driving by herself throughout the
metropolitan area.

Exposure to panic.   The cognitive therapy model of panic
disorder is that the patient fears most a panic attack. Consequently, it is considered desirable that she actually experience
a panic attack in order to learn how to decatastrophize, correctly label, and cope with the sensations. As already indicated, panickers believe that their panic is awful, escalating,
dangerous, and intolerable. The goal in treatment is to help the
patient understand that her feelings are simply arousal or
collapse sensations that can be offset by simple techniques.

For example, David Clark's (1986) cognitive therapy of
panic is used with hyperventilators. The patient who hyper-
ventilates is told that when he feels short of breath he tends to
breathe more rapidly and exhale too much CO_2. As a result, his
CO_2 balance is off, leading to more overbreathing. This results
in sensations of dizziness and collapse. (Before patients are
involved in this procedure, they should receive medical clear-

ance from their physician.) The patient is asked to stand, breathe rapidly for several minutes, and report the sensations he is having. The therapist asks, "Are these sensations similar to your panic symptoms?" The patient is then told to breathe into a paper bag (or into his hands), or to run in place, thereby restoring the proper CO_2 balance. Dramatically for these patients, their panic attack has been induced and eliminated in just a few minutes. Because the patient now recognizes what causes and escalates his panic and how he can reduce it, there is less to be feared. Anticipatory anxiety and avoidance, as well as the frequency of panic attacks, are often drastically reduced.

Cognitive treatment of panic has been shown to be extremely effective (see McNally [1994] for a review). In the course of fifteen to twenty sessions without medication, 75 to 90 percent of patients show improvement—often maintaining their gains (even increasing their improvement) on two-year follow-up.

OBSESSIVE-COMPULSIVE DISORDER

Obsessive-compulsive disorder is characterized by recurring thoughts or images associated with increased anxiety. As anxiety increases, the individual is motivated to decrease the anxiety by engaging in neutralizing behavioral or mental activity, such as rituals or attempts to replace the disturbing obsessive thought with a neutral thought or image. For example, obsessions about contamination are neutralized by behavioral rituals, such as washing, which attempt to rid the individual of the contamination. These rituals help reduce anxiety and are, therefore, reinforced. As the patient experiences anxiety reduction through the performance of rituals he or she learns that other experiences of anxiety may be reduced by compulsive ritualization.

Typical obsessions include thoughts or images about aggression, contamination, sexual acting out, religious blasphemy, and other behavior perceived by the patient as dangerous or inappropriate. The occurrence of the thought or image is upsetting to the patient, even though he may realize on reflection that the thought or fear is irrational.

Consider the following case of a 32-year-old married heterosexual male who had been seen in psychodynamic therapy intermittently since age 13. When he was a young teenager he was referred to his family priest for counseling, due to his worries and "oversensitivity." The priest was someone he trusted and admired but who attempted a homosexual seduction of the young boy. This set off a long history of obsessions: "I must be gay! I can't stand the idea that I could be gay." As a consequence of the fear that he might be homosexual, he avoided eye contact with men and felt the need to leave the room if there were any gay men present. As an adult, if he had difficulty performing sexually with his wife, he would think, "This must mean I'm gay." The patient denied any history of homosexual behavior or fantasy and was intolerant of any signs of homosexuality in himself. Other obsessions appeared intermittently: "I could get so angry I could hurt my wife" or "My anxiety might lead me to go crazy."

The patient would neutralize these obsessions by praying, avoiding eye contact, leaving the room or house if there were gay people present or if he got angry with his wife, self-critical statements ("Stop worrying! What's wrong with you!"), and exaggerated "macho" posing ("one of the guys"). These neutralizations were both cognitive and behavioral compulsions that served the purpose of temporarily relieving his anxiety but also reinforced his belief that his thoughts and feelings were dangerous. By the time he entered cognitive therapy, he felt hopeless, alone, depressed and suicidal.

The patient was instructed in the cognitive model of obsessive-compulsive disorder (OCD). Ironically, despite his years of therapy, he had never been told that he was obsessive-compulsive. The author recommended Foa and Wilson's excellent self-help book, *Stop Obsessing* (1991), as well as publications from the OCD Foundation in Milford, Connecticut. (The OCD Foundation is an excellent information source for OCD patients, providing monthly newsletters, recommended readings, and brochures explaining OCD. Most important, they help the OCD patient realize that he or she is not alone.)

A small percentage of OCD patients have overvalued ideas, obsessions they believe are rational, but are patently absurd to a reasonable person: "I could have gotten AIDS by touching the subway pole." The therapist should always ask patients if they believe that their worries are reasonable and rational. Some authors (Marks 1987) have compared overvalued ideas to monodelusions. Patients with overvalued ideas generally do not respond well to behavioral treatments. However, the therapist may overcome this resistance by submitting these ideas to cognitive therapy evaluation (Salkovskis and Kirk 1989). We recommend examining all obsessions for reasonableness in order to rule out overvalued ideas as well as to enhance the efficacy of behavioral techniques.

Returning to the patient who worried about homosexuality, I had him define both homosexual and heterosexual traits. We examined the advantages and disadvantages of worrying about his homosexuality (or violent tendencies or going crazy). Like many obsessives, he believed that an advantage of worrying about these problems was that he could catch himself and prevent his acting out. He had never engaged in homosexuality, had never acted violently with any women, and had never gone crazy, so there was an illusory correlation, since he had worried about these things but they really had never happened.

I told him that obsessives almost always worry about the quality least characteristic and most unacceptable to them. This conflicted with his assumption that his obsessiveness was an indication of what was ultimately *most* characteristic of him. We then examined the evidence for and against his idea that he was homosexual; all of the evidence pointed to his heterosexuality. Similarly, we challenged his idea that he was violent or insane.

Next, I recommended setting aside thirty minutes per day when he would sit at his desk and worry intensely. He was told to write down as many worries as he could. The purpose of this was to set the worries into a limited time–place frame, rather than spend the entire day worrying everywhere.

I compared his obsessions with a fear of elevators: the only way to get over a fear of elevators was to get on the elevator. He was asked to rate his subjective units of distress (SUDS) (anxiety), from 0 to 10, with 0 corresponding to the absence of any anxiety and 10 corresponding to panic. I also asked him how anxious he felt when he had obsessions about homosexuality, and he replied that his level of anxiety often reached 9 or 10. The next task was to practice exposure to the obsession during the session without neutralization, such as praying, distracting, reassurance seeking, or even rational responding. He was asked to repeat, slowly and with focus, "Maybe I am gay," and to indicate after every twenty repetitions of this phrase his SUDS (distress).

The rationale for exposure to the obsession is that repetition of the obsession without distraction would lead to habituation. The stimulus, "I am gay," would lose its strength to elicit an emotional response. Furthermore, by maintaining exposure without escape or avoidance, he would learn that the thought itself was not dangerous. Early in such exposures, his SUDS reached a level of 9 (very high anxiety, almost panic), but with repetition, the SUDS declined to 2. Eventually he indicated that the thought was getting boring, and I responded that he was getting better: "Boredom is the opposite of anxious."

Homework included thirty minutes per day of repeating his

feared obsessions. He was not allowed to seek reassurance from anyone for his worries, since reassurance serves as a mental compulsion that neutralizes and, thereby, reinforces the obsession. He was further instructed that whenever he had any obsession in the course of the day, he was to repeat the obsession at least 100 times.

Like many OCD patients, this individual improved rapidly, much to his surprise, since he was engaged in the counter-intuitive behavior of increasing the frequency of his obsession.

A note on thought stopping: although many behavior therapists have recommended the use of thought stopping for obsessions, the outcome data do not support this as an effective treatment. In fact in many cases there is evidence of a rebound effect—the initial suppression of an unwanted thought can lead to a subsequent increase in that thought. For example, try not to think of pink elephants. Thought stopping also reinforces the cognition that the patient cannot tolerate the thought or feeling. One can argue that thought stopping, as a distraction, may serve the purpose of a mental ritual or compulsion (Wegner 1989).

Behavioral compulsions. Traditionally, clinicians have distinguished between obsessions as thoughts or images and compulsions as overt behavior. For example, the thought, "I am contaminated," is followed by the behavioral compulsion of handwashing. However, as already indicated, the mental obsession "I am gay," may be followed by mental compulsions—praying, self-statements, even images of heterosexual behavior. Consequently, behavioral therapists now distinguish between mental and behavioral rituals or compulsions.

Behavioral therapy for an OCD patient with behavioral rituals is relatively straightforward. Therapy consists of exposure with response prevention. The patient who fears contamination and neutralizes those fears by washing his hands for twenty minutes fifteen times per day will be asked to soil his hands with dirt and refrain from washing for several hours. Patients with apparently senseless rituals (walking in and out of the door ten times) will be required to walk through the door once, stand on the other side for fifteen minutes, and continue on without returning. The key rule is that the patient must confront the feared stimulus that elicits the compulsion and be prevented from carrying out the compulsion.

Needless to say, gaining patient commitment and compliance with the treatment program is not always easy. The patient must be told what the rationale is for treatment (see Foa and Wilson 1991). The patient must also be told that during the course of therapy, he or she will be required to do things to provoke anxiety, but the goal is for the exposure to lead to a decrease in anxiety. Since in vitro or in vivo exposure needs to be repeated many times in order for the patient to become habituated to the feared stimulus, we recommend double sessions two or three times per week during the initial three weeks of overexposure. This massed practice both dramatically confronts the anxiety stimuli and dramatically reduces the anxiety. Consequently, patient commitment to this intense but actually brief treatment package is important. Half-hearted attempts at exposure and response prevention only dilute the efficacy of the treatment and further allow the patient to resensitize to the feared stimulus between sessions.

Patients who find total response prevention (abstinence) to be too difficult may be requested to engage in response modification. This may include response delay ("See if you can go fifteen minutes without washing your hands.") or variation of the response ("Try walking in and out of the door no more than three times."). The advantage of response modification over abstinence is that some patients may find this more palatable, and there may be more compliance. However, research comparing response modification with response abstinence indicates that the latter technique is more effective (Steketee

1993). The clinician must judge whether the client is willing to go all the way with response prevention.

With patients for whom the feared stimulus or image is highly improbable, making direct exposure and response prevention impossible, we recommend imaginal exposure. In this technique, the patient is exposed to a narrative describing in gruesome detail the feared events. Patients with a fear of contamination are given a detailed description of how contamination will lead to their death. Details of their funeral are given, complete with guilt-inducing statements such as "Everyone is thinking how you could have prevented this from happening, but you were so careless." The therapist must use caution and skill in telling the patient that the purpose of imaginal exposure is to expose him to a feared stimulus, while preventing escape or neutralization. He should be told that the imagery will be anxiety provoking, but its repeated exposure will lead to anxiety reduction. The feared imagery should then be repeated to the patient for thirty to forty-five minutes, with intermittent judgments of SUDS given by the patient. Once patients confront and habituate to their worst fears, the obsessions and compulsions are reduced.

A note on the use of relaxation training: although it is almost always a useful adjunct for patients with anxiety, the relaxation exercise should not be paired with the obsession. Consider the patient with a fear of homosexuality. If he were instructed to have the obsession, but to pair it with relaxation, the relaxation response would serve as an escape or neutralization ritual. This would further reinforce the patient's belief that the thought "Maybe I am gay," has to be neutralized. The goal is to demonstrate to the patient that the thought is not dangerous and can be tolerated. Perhaps this is why research indicates that combining relaxation training with the techniques described here does not add significantly to rates of improvement in patients with OCD.

CONCLUSION

In 1975 cognitive behavioral therapy provided only limited techniques for the clinician in the treatment of anxiety disorders. At that time, emphasis in treatment was on relaxation training, thought stopping, and floo ing. Today the cognitive behavioral therapist has a significant range of techniques from which to draw, and the conceptualization of panic, agoraphobia, and obsessive-compulsive disorder can now be based on newer models. The efficacy of cognitive techniques in the treatment of anxiety disorders is clearly established, with many patients who have suffered for years benefiting after a few months of treatment. Given the fact that anxiety disorders are the most prevalent—and more long lasting than depressive disorders—these intervention techniques should prove helpful to all clinicians, independent of their theoretical orientation.

9

MARITAL THERAPY

Marital, or relationship conflict, is the single most common complaint among women patients presenting with depression. For many patients, marital therapy is as effective as anti-depressant medication or individual therapy in the relief of depression. The added benefit of marital therapy is that both the depression and the marital discord are improved (Beach et al. 1992). Although divorce may often prove to be the more desirable alternative, the clinician should not underestimate the pervasive negative impact of divorce on subsequent coping. Divorced spouses show elevations in depression, anxiety, substance abuse, smoking, and poverty. Furthermore, the children of divorce fare poorly, showing increased truancy, school problems, depression, and lowered self-esteem. It is in this context that we view marital therapy as an important component of the comprehensive treatment of the patient.

RELATIONSHIP MODELS

The cognitive approach to marital conflict is based on several complementary models of relationships. The behavioral model proposes that marital conflict is a consequence of deficits in reinforcements and increased aversive experiences. For example, Gottman (1995) proposes that marital satisfaction is based on achieving a ratio of five positives for every negative. Individuals who perceive themselves as receiving negatives from their partners may feel that the negatives are offset by the positives. Behavioral models also include social exchange models that propose each partner weigh his or her relative inputs to received rewards and compare these ratios with alternatives. Simply put, each partner asks, "Am I getting back what I put in?" and "Could I get a better payoff elsewhere?" Behavioral models that emphasize reward/punishment ratios are the basis of therapeutic interventions that encourage couples to increase positives, increase the perception of positives, ignore negatives in the partner, and decrease negatives by the self.

Communication models of marital conflict, such as Stuart (1980) and Guerney (1977), view marital conflict as resulting from inadequate or dysfunctional communication and listening skills. These therapeutic models emphasize training couples in communication skills, such as responsible assertiveness, editing, and non-accusatory speech, and in assisting couples in learning active listening skills, such as rephrasing, inquiry, empathy, and validation.

The cognitive model, derived from Beck's theory, proposes that marital dysfunction is a result of inaccuracies in information processing and rigid assumptions and rules (Beck and Freeman 1990, Datillio and Padesky 1990, Baucom and Epstein 1990). According to these theorists, marital conflict arises from the individual's automatic thought distortions, such as mind reading, personalizing, and catastrophizing. These distortions are further exacerbated by rigid and perfectionist rules or underlying assumptions that intensify the individual's negative affect or elicit negative behavior.

This chapter will describe interventions based on the behavioral, communication, and cognitive models. In clinical practice most cognitive therapists integrate these three models and may on occasion include individual consultations and individual therapy along with conjoint therapy.

BEHAVIORAL INTERVENTIONS

Increasing rewards. The hallmark of satisfying relationships is for each partner to experience important rewards in the relationship. Often distressed couples will decrease rewarding behavior because they feel they are not receiving rewards from each other. This follows the rule of reciprocity in relationships—you give what you get. Thus, if you are rewarded, you will probably reward your spouse. Similarly, if you are punished, you will probably punish your spouse either through withdrawal or criticism. The unfortunate outcome for distressed couples is that as one spouse decreases rewards, the other spouse responds in kind, thereby confirming their belief that the relationship is unrewarding. The first set of interventions focuses on assisting the partners in identifying rewarding behavior.

Each partner is asked to indicate which behaviors during the last week were pleasurable for the self. Couples are told that distressed partners are often "negative trackers" (Jacobson and Margolin 1980) and that the purpose of the first exercises is to assist in catching your partner being good. Each is told to be specific about behaviors of the other rather than make vague statements such as, "You were nice last night." The first homework assignment involves each partner making a list of several positives per day and bringing that to the next session. In addition, each spouse is asked to make a wish list of positives that he or she would like to see more of, with the stipulation that these preferred behaviors must be relatively easy, not time consuming and not expensive. The wish list is then used to assign caring or pleasure days, with each partner assigned one day during the following week during which he or she must engage in some of the behaviors on the partner's wish list. Often, the effect of these early interventions is to enhance the positive affect of the couple.

Each is urged to attend, label, and reward the positives in the partner. Attending is increased by the exercise in positive tracking already described. Labeling entails accurate behavioral descriptions of the partner's positive behavior, and rewarding involves an overt verbal or physical behavior that conveys approval. For example, the wife can attend, label, and reward the husband's efforts at preparing dinner by saying, "I really like it when you make dinner" with an affectionate hug attached to her statement. The value of attending, labeling, and rewarding is that the partner who is so rewarded will feel appreciated and learn the kinds of behaviors that will gain approval.

We recommend that couples try to "catch your spouse" engaging in three positives each day, and writing down exactly what happened and how they felt. For example, Ellen noticed the following positives (see Table 9–1).

At the end of the week, spouses meet at home and read off what they noticed that was positive. Each spouse might be

Table 9–1. Positive Tracking (Monday)

Spouse's Behavior	How I Felt
Talked with me about the kids	Good, like we were partners
Made tea for me	Happy; I felt cared for
Watched TV with me	Content; we were together

surprised that many of the things that he or she did were noticed and were rewarding. Interestingly, partners often do not really know what their spouses like.

Assign Caring Days

Each partner is asked, "What would you like your spouse to do that you might find rewarding?" We suggest partners make up wish lists—a list of ten or fifteen behaviors they would like their spouse to carry out in less than twenty minutes at little or no financial cost. The rules are that either spouse can refuse to do any or all things on the list "as long as you both come up with a list of ten behaviors. Each of you is assigned a caring day in the next week during which you will give pleasure to your spouse, selecting items from that list."

The purpose of this exercise is to inform the spouse, assert desires, and experience giving and obtaining pleasure. Interestingly, some partners have difficulty identifying specific behaviors that would please them. Often partners believe that pleasure can only be obtained from unusual, special, or romantic behaviors, rather than from the many rewarding but mundane behaviors of daily life. Further, when the therapist points out some things that one spouse did that appeared positive, the intended recipient of the reward may often discredit the behavior ("That's what wives should do") or zap the spouse ("You did it this week. Why didn't you do it in the past?"). Finally, this exercise can also assess each partner's willingness to reward the other.

Mutual Problem Solving

Some marital therapists have argued that much marital conflict is a result of poor problem-solving skills. As important as problem solving may be, our clinical experience suggests that the use of punitive or angry coercive patterns, failures in communication and listening skills, and maladaptive assumptions are key impediments to progress. Many spouses actually have good problem-solving and assertive skills, but they do not see them as relevant to the problems at hand in their marriage. Consequently, we focus the initial sessions on increasing rewards, decreasing negatives, improving communication skills, and cognitive therapy before we move on to mutual problem solving. The reason for this is that mutual problem solving is often unnecessary for couples who can reward and communicate well.

The first step is to identify the problem that refers to manageable behavior. In this case, the wife will bring up the problem of planning events together. According to Jacobson and Margolin (1980), the steps in mutual problem solving are:

1. Identify the problem as "our" problem.
   "I think we have a problem planning things together."
2. Ask your spouse if he/she would be willing to help in solving the problem.
   "Would you be willing to talk with me about how we can make this better?"
3. Work on only one problem. (Avoid getting side-tracked by other problems that may come up).
   "That's an important problem. Perhaps we can get to that after we solve this problem."
4. Identify your own role in the problem.
   "I can certainly see how I've contributed to the problem. I haven't made much of an effort to tell you what I like."
5. Brainstorm but don't make judgments about any possible solutions.
   "Let's see how many possible solutions we can come up with at this point."

6. Go over the possible solutions. Each of you should prioritize (from most attractive to not acceptable) the possible solutions.

    "Let's each rate these alternatives and see how we feel about them."

7. Be willing to compromise. There is no ultrasolution—only a middle ground that works a little for you and a little for your spouse. Select a solution you both find acceptable.

    " I can see the merit in a lot of these ideas."

8. Set up an experiment with your agreed-upon solution.

    "Let's set up a plan and try out one of our solutions."

9. Carry out your experiment. (The couple carries out the plan and evaluates the outcome.)

10. Revise the solution or try a different solution if the first one didn't work.

    "Let's look at how we did with our plan last week. Maybe we can improve on it."

11. Reward each other for working together as partners.

    "I really appreciate your cooperation in doing this. It looks like you're trying."

The advantage of the problem-solving model is that it focuses the couple on proactive strategies and behaviors rather than on complaining about the past. D'Zurilla (1986) has found that training individuals and couples in problem solving skills is helpful in reducing depression, anxiety, and marital conflict.

Although problem solving is practical, solutions are not always the goal for partners in conflict. Communication models of marital discord emphasize the importance of empathy, warmth, and understanding, independent of whether specific problems are solved. In fact men may be overly focused on solving problems while women are more interested in connecting with feelings and ideas.

COMMUNICATION MODELS

Gottman (1995), Guerney (1977), Markman (1984), and Stuart (1980) have all proposed that relationship dysfunction is often the result of inadequate or faulty communication patterns. Recent popular books on relationship conflict, such as Deborah Tannen's (1990) *You Just Don't Understand*, propose that men and women often differ in the style and purposes of communication, further contributing to marital discord. Here we will review interventions that may be useful in improving the communication and listening skills of both partners, and how stylistic differences in communication can be bridged.

Guerney's (1977) relationship enhancement model is specifically an educational model of intervention. He views the therapist as one who can educate the client about how dysfunction arises and provides him with the skills to deal with it. According to Guerney, couples view compassion and understanding as desirable goals, and although many marital partners may agree with this view, our observation is that resistance is a powerful impediment to the use of relationship enhancement skills. Consequently, cognitive techniques to counter the resistance are often required in marital therapy.

Guerney distinguishes between the expressive mode and the empathic responder mode. The expressive mode is equivalent to the speaker, while the empathic responder is the listener, the one who is in a receptive frame of mind, who is focused on understanding how the other partner perceives events. The empathic responder attempts to show his or her interest in the partner's message and feelings. Guerney provides rules for listening: do not ask for new information, do not present your opinion, do not interpret events for the speaker, do not offer suggestions, and do not judge.

The expressor (speaker) mode is characterized by acting as if "you are the world's authority on everything you say" (Guerney 1977, p. 29). Moroever, the speaker should express his or her views as if they were subjective: "I believe that you are neglecting me." The expressor should describe his or her feelings associated with thoughts or events: "I am angry when you read the newspaper while we are eating." But the expressor should find something positive to say, even when offering a criticism: "I know you want the place to be clean, too, so I hope that you'll do your share of the housework." The expressor should also be as specific and behavioral as possible, avoiding overgeneralizations such as "You're messy."

Communication difficulties often arise because of the difference between the speaker's intention and the impact of what is said. Intention is defined as the message the speaker believes he or she is communicating, whereas impact is defined as the message the listener hears or receives. The listener is instructed by the therapist to attempt to focus all of his or her attention on the content and feelings of the speaker's message, to try to apprehend the intention of the speaker. The partner who is functioning as an active listener is instructed to rephrase, empathize, validate, and inquire.

Rephrasing means repeating back to the speaker what the listener is hearing or the content of the message: *Listener:* "What you are saying is that I do not include you in decisions."

Empathizing refers to the recognition of the feelings or emotions communicated by the speaker: *Listener:* "You're saying that this makes you feel ignored and angry. "

Validating refers to the listener's attempt to find some truth in the speaker's message, usually by trying to take the other's perspective. *Listener:* "I can see why it would make you angry if you believed that I didn't include you in decisions. I can see how my behavior would sometimes lead you to think this."

Finally, *inquiry* refers to the listener's attempt to gather more information on the speaker's point of view: *Listener:* Can you tell me some other ways in which you feel that I do not include you in decision making?

In order to verify that the listener is understanding the speaker's message, the listener may ask for feedback: "Am I rephrasing you correctly?" or "Do I seem to understand how you are feeling?" or "Is there something I am missing?" If the speaker believes the listener is missing part of the message, she can expand on her message or correct the listener. While the partner is in the listener role, she can enhance her impact as listener by using nonverbal communication, such as maintaining eye contact, touching the speaker's hand, sitting close to or facing the speaker, nodding her head, and using facial expressions.

As already indicated, the active listener is truly active. Many people believe they are effective listeners simply because they sit passively and absorb or remember information. The foregoing examples emphasize the interactive-communicative nature of listening, with the listener providing continual feedback to the speaker.

Partners in couples therapy are shown how to play the role of speaker and listener in sessions with the therapist alternating both roles with each partner. Each partner then takes the speaker or listener role in session and the therapist intervenes when necessary. Listeners are instructed not to defend, explain, promise, argue, or try to fix the problem. Speakers are told to limit their message to no more than two minutes per communication; this gives the listener an opportunity to respond. (Some speakers can deliver long-winded speeches that lead to loss of interest and boredom on the listener's part. Consequently, time limits are valuable.) The couple is told to practice the active-listener exercise at home three times for twenty minutes during the next week and tape-record the exercise for review during the next session. Each partner is told to occupy the speaker role for no more than ten minutes.

Building common ground. A useful variation of the active-listener exercise can follow after the speaker has talked for his ten minutes; he can then ask the listener if there is agreement

on any part. Building common ground is one of the fundamental principles of any negotiation. We often find that couples are amazed at how much they agree on. The speaker can
then ask the listener where she disagrees and if this is truly a
disagreement or simply a misunderstanding of his position.
These interventions are quite powerful at reducing conflict,
since many couples are often arguing about different issues
simultaneously.

Marital Styles

Individuals differ considerably in their ability to tolerate conflict. Gottman (1995) divides marital styles into conflict avoidant, volatile, and validator. Interestingly, each marital style
can work under the right conditions, but unfortunately partners often differ in their styles. A husband may be conflict-
avoidant while the wife may be a validator: he wants to limit
conflictual interactions, whereas she wants to talk things
through. Gottman and others have found that men show extreme physiological arousal during interpersonal conflict and
may withdraw from conflict simply to reduce this arousal. If
the wife is focused on validation—being heard, understood,
and working problems through—she will interpret his withdrawal as not caring.
   Volatile couples place considerable emphasis on expres-
siveness, honesty, spontaneity, and "being myself." These
relationships are sometimes characterized by very positive
feelings, but can often (and quickly) revert to extreme negative
feelings. As a consequence of the higher negativity of volatile
relationships, Gottman indicates there is a corresponding
greater need for a high frequency and intensity of positives.
   He also suggests that couples must first identify their individual styles and preferences and then negotiate rules or an
understanding of which style they wish to adopt. Popular

books on socio-linguistic differences (especially sex differences), such as Deborah Tannen's (1990) excellent, *You Just Don't Understand*, are helpful in illustrating communication styles. Once partners see that their problems are due to a difference in style rather than rejection, it is often easier to intervene with communication exercises and rules for resolving conflict.

Rules for Arguing

Gottman (1995) identifies four styles of communication that are predictive of marital dysfunction and divorce—criticism, contempt, defensiveness, and stonewalling. Criticism involves attacking the personal qualities of the other person. Contempt includes attempts to insult or psychologically abuse the spouse by insults, name-calling, hostile humor, and mockery. Defensiveness includes denying responsibility, making excuses, negative mind reading, cross-complaining, rubber man/woman (e.g., "You said X," "Yeah, but you did Y"), yes-butting, repeating oneself, whining, and negative body language. Stonewalling involves withdrawal, refusal to interact, and silence. Gottman finds that these styles are highly predictive of divorce and marital dysfunction.

I have found it useful to present couples with rules (see Table 9–2) for arguing that can help them avoid the escalation of conflict.

Following these rules is not always possible for highly distressed couples. In couples where hostility or violence has erupted, it is necessary to use time-out procedures to cool down the irate partner.

Anger Control

Anger in itself is neither good nor bad in relationships, but it is inevitable. The issue, however, is whether anger is excessive

Table 9-2. Rules for Arguing

DO	DON'T
Present the difference as a problem to be solved by both.	Bring up past wrongs.
	Bring up irrelevant material.
Stick to one simple topic.	Label your spouse.
Stay in the present.	Ask, "Why do you always. . . ?"
Indicate your own role in the problem; accept some responsibility.	Pout.
	Threaten.
	Raise your voice.
Invite your spouse to solve the problem with you.	Try to be affectionate when your spouse is disagreeing with you.
Ask your spouse if he or she has some ideas about solutions.	Be sarcastic.
	Whine.
Suggest some points of agreement.	Interpret your spouse's motives.
Propose that you try one solution that both of you agree on.	Try to win.
	Try to make your spouse seem foolish.

and whether its expression proves to be destructive. Many people incorrectly believe that it is necessary or desirable to ventilate anger, since they view anger as part of a hydraulic system that needs expression or release. The cognitive model recognizes that it is often important to inform others of the self's negative feelings, but the degree of anger and the style of its expression are key elements in marital therapy.

We distinguish between anger and hostility. Anger is the negative feeling that arises when one is frustrated or insulted, whereas hostility involves behaviors that are expressed with the intention of harming others. It is important for patients to recognize that anger need not lead to an expression of hostility. In fact the arousal of anger may be a good signal to attempt active listening skills, responsible assertion, time-out, correction of automatic thought distortions, or mutual problem solving.

Typical automatic thought distortions underlying anger are catastrophizing ("It's awful that my husband nagged me!" and "I can't stand it"), labeling ("She's neurotic"), personalizing ("He only does this with me"), mind reading ("She thinks she can make me look like a fool"), fortune telling ("He's going to criticize me"), all-or-nothing thinking ("This is always happening"), and discounting positives ("The only reason she's acting better is that the therapist told her to change"). Angry spouses may be overly focused on assumptions that are unrealistic and rigid, such as needing approval for everything ("If my spouse doesn't agree with me, she is not to be trusted" or "It means he thinks I'm a fool") and perfectionism ("Our relationship should be free from conflict" or "Marriage should be easy"). Identifying and correcting these automatic thoughts and assumptions are essential in overcoming a couple's resistance to change.

Anger is often the result of the individual's perception that he or she is threatened, insulted, or frustrated in the pursuit of goals that are believed important. As Beck (in press) indicates, anger often results from a belief that the self is threatened, either in losing resources, esteem, or status. The husband may express jealous anger because he perceives his status as threatened by other males, he views his wife's behavior as insulting to him, and he believes that he will be blocked in pursuing his relationship with his wife. Angry cognitive distortions include personalization ("She's making a fool of me"), labeling ("She can't be trusted"), mind reading ("She thinks I'm weak"), catastrophizing ("It's awful when she's not focused on me"), and overgeneralization ("This happens all the time"). The angry spouse often subscribes to a variety of "should" statements: "My wife should never show an interest in talking to other men" or "My husband should make me feel special and unique." As Dodge and Coie (1987) and others have shown, angry and hostile individuals are more likely than others to perceive provocation.

I have proposed (Leahy 1993) that hostile interactions are often attempts to obtain confirmation for a pre-existing cognition. For example, the husband believes his wife will not discuss problems rationally. Based on this assumption he provokes her by labeling her as overly emotional, thereby eliciting the very behavior to which he objects. Due to his tendency to ascribe negative outcomes to others, he blames his wife for the emotional behavior he both predicted and provoked. Another sociocognitive process arises when the husband, recognizing the untenability of his position, provokes the wife in order to have an advantage over her, so he can now point to her negative behavior and distract the interaction from evaluating his behavior. I refer to this (Leahy 1993) as a transfer of the problem: the couple now will focus on the wife's reaction, rather than the husband's initial behavior.

Spouses often have secondary assumptions that guide them to translate their anger into overt hostile behavior. The primary assumptions are those rules that elicit the anger in the first place: "My wife should understand my needs without my telling her." The secondary assumption is that "I should punish people who frustrate me." The cognitive therapist needs to examine both sets of assumptions—those that arouse anger and those that lead to hostility.

People often hold to hostile assumptions because they believe that without hostility they will be worse off. Hostile assumptions include the rationale for acting against the partner: "I need to teach him a lesson. I need to make him feel like I do. Then he will understand and he'll change. I need to raise the cost for him so that he won't do that again. If I don't express my hostility, I will become depressed. I have a right to my anger."

Angry and hostile spouses are reluctant to change their anger despite its obvious dysfunctionality. The first step in modifying anger and hostility is to label those emotions and behaviors and for the patient to examine the costs and benefits of hostility. Hostility has a high degree of reciprocity (negatives lead to negatives by your spouse), guilt, hopelessness, and dissolution. It is remarkable how many extremely hostile spouses seem so unaware that their partners actually might leave. It may be useful to examine with each spouse the costs and benefits of divorce, not only to raise the motivation to modify the hostility, but also to examine if divorce is a desirable alternative. In the treatment of very angry and hostile partners we recommend the use of time-out procedures early on.

RULES FOR TIME-OUT

We tell partners: "If you and your spouse are explosive in your arguing or if you have experienced violence in your relationship, use time-out when you feel very angry. Tell your partner that you need to go to another room for at least fifteen minutes. If your partner asks for time out, don't follow him. Use the time to challenge your angry thoughts and to plan a more adaptive way to express your needs. When you return, consider the following rules":

1. Either partner may call for a time-out.
2. When time-out is announced, it is preferable that you go to separate rooms for fifteen minutes to cool down.
3. Do not follow your partner into time-out. Do not talk with her or provoke her.
4. Think it through in time-out.
5. While you are cooling down during the fifteen minutes, write down your automatic thoughts.
6. Are you using any of the cognitive distortions described earlier? Are you labeling ("He's just selfish and mean"),

mind reading and personalizing ("She's trying to make me look like a fool"), or catastrophizing ("I can't stand it when he's this way")?

7. Challenge your automatic thoughts. Is there evidence that he's not always selfish and mean? Could it be that she's simply explaining her feelings and thoughts rather than trying to make you look like an idiot?

8. What are your hidden assumptions and shoulds? For example, are you inordinately concerned about her approval? Do you think that he has to agree with everything you say? Do you think you should always get your way?

9. Return to your spouse and acknowledge your role in the problem. Suggest that you move on to mutual problem-solving.

These rules, when accompanied by active-listening exercises, help reduce the likelihood of criticism, contempt, defensiveness, and stonewalling. The therapist who is treating a couple in which one or both partners display extreme anger will want to set anger reduction as the initial focus of therapy. As experienced clinicians know, attempts to modify anger are often met with resistance: angry partners externalize the problem with claims that it's always the other person's fault. When the therapist challenges the angry spouse, he may turn against the therapist: "You're taking her side" or "You don't understand how I feel." As valuable as the behavioral and communication models are, cognitive interventions are often useful to the therapist in addressing the underlying resistance to change.

COGNITIVE MODEL

The cognitive model stresses the importance of correcting the automatic thought distortions frequently found in distressed couples. Individuals in interaction often have very different interpretations of events. The depressed spouse may see rejection, loss, emptiness, and hopelessness; the anxious spouse may focus on perceived threats of abandonment or future failure or humiliation; and the angry spouse may personalize, feel provoked, and perceive humiliation. We have already referred to a variety of these cognitive distortions in our discussion of anger control.

Cognitive interventions are often useful not only in reducing negative emotion, but also in addressing the patient's resistance to change. As we illustrate below, the patient's underlying assumptions and schemas are often central impediments to the utilization of positive behavioral and communication techniques. Here we review the automatic thought distortions, maladaptive assumptions, and schemas that underlie marital discord and examine a number of treatment recommendations for modifying these cognitive distortions.

AUTOMATIC THOUGHT DISTORTIONS FOR COUPLES

1. *Labeling.* You attribute a negative personality trait to your spouse leading you to believe that he or she can never change. "He's passive-aggressive." "She's neurotic."

2. *Fortune telling.* You forecast the future and predict things will never get better, leaving you feeling helpless and hopeless. "He'll never change. I'll always be unhappy in my marriage."

3. *Mind reading.* You interpret the motivations of your spouse as hostile or selfish on the basis of very little evidence. "You don't care how I feel." "You're saying that because you're trying to get back at me."

4. *Catastrophic thinking.* You treat conflict or problems as if they indicate that the world has ended or that your marriage

is awful. "It's awful that we have these arguments." "I can't stand her nagging." "It's awful that we haven't had sex recently."

5. *Emotional reasoning.* You feel depressed and anxious and you conclude that your emotions indicate your marriage is a failure. "We must have a terrible marriage because I'm unhappy." "I don't have the same feelings toward him that I used to, so I guess we're no longer in love."

6. *Negative filter.* You focus on the few negative experiences in your relationship and fail to recognize or recall the positives. You probably bring up past history in a series of complaints that sounds like you're putting your spouse on trial. "You were rude to me last week." "You talked to that other person and ignored me entirely."

7. *All-or-nothing thinking.* You describe your interactions as being all good or all bad without examining the possibility that some experiences with your spouse are positive. "You're never kind to me." "You never show affection." "You're always negative."

8. *Discounting the positive.* You may recognize that positives do exist, but disregard them by saying: "That's what a wife or husband should do." "Well, so he did do that—it means nothing." "These are trivial things you're talking about."

9. *Perfectionism.* You hold up a standard for a relationship that is unrealistically high and then compare your relationship to this standard. "It's not like it was in the first year, so it's not worth it." "My wife (husband) should make me happy all the time."

10. *Personalizing.* You attribute your partner's moods and behavior to something you've done or you take all the blame for the problems. "He's in a bad mood because of me." "If it weren't for me, we wouldn't have these problems."

11. *Externalization of responsibility.* You believe that the problems in the relationship are out of your control. "If it weren't for her, we wouldn't have these problems." "He argues with me and that's why we can't get along."

In addition to these cognitive distortions, distressed partners often display rigid, moralistic, and impossible assumptions or rules that contribute to feelings of hopelessness and increased conflict. Several of these should statements, if–then rules, or assumptions are indicated in Table 9–3.

Changing Automatic Thoughts and Assumptions

The cognitive therapist assists the patient in identifying and challenging distressing thoughts and assumptions. She can ask each partner the following questions:

1. Identify your automatic thoughts when you are angry, anxious, or sad. (Are you saying to yourself, "He doesn't love me" or "Everything is going wrong in my marriage"?)

Table 9–3. Maladaptive Assumptions Used by Couples

"My spouse should always know what I want without my asking."
"If my spouse doesn't do what I want her to do, I should punish her."
"I should never be unhappy (bored, angry, etc.) with my spouse."
"I shouldn't have to work at a relationship; it should come naturally."
"Talking about these things just makes them worse."
"My spouse should change first."
"It's all his fault, so why should I change?"
"If I don't get my way, I should complain (pout, withdraw, give up)."
"Our sex life should always be fantastic."
"If I'm attracted to other people, it means that I shouldn't stay in this marriage."
"I should try to win in all of our conflicts."
"My spouse should accept me just the way I am."
"If we're having problems it means we have an awful relationship."
"I shouldn't have to wait for change; it should come immediately."

2. What cognitive distortions are you using? (Are you mind reading or using all-or-nothing thinking?)

3. What are the advantages and disadvantages to your thought? (Are there any benefits to believing your partner doesn't love you? What are the costs of this thought? Does it make you feel hopeless, alone, or angry?)

4. What if your thought is true? (Do you think you are unlovable if your partner doesn't love you at this moment? Does this mean your life lacks any reward or meaning?)

5. What is the evidence for and against your thinking? (List the evidence for and against your thought. Are you concluding that based on a few behaviors your partner doesn't love you? Are there ways in which he or she shows love?)

6. What are your underlying assumptions? Your "should" statements? (Are you saying to yourself, "He doesn't love me because he doesn't respond exactly the way I wish he would"? Are you saying to yourself, "She should always do what I want" or "If our sex life is not great, then she doesn't love me"?)

7. If you had a friend with this problem, what would you advise her to do? (Try to step outside of the situation and imagine yourself giving advice to a friend on how to handle a similar problem.)

8. Are there less negative explanations for your partner's behavior? (Perhaps there are more neutral explanations for what is going on. Perhaps your partner is tired, bothered by other things, not intending you harm, or feeling misunderstood. Perhaps you are observing something temporary or situational, something that may change if you change your behavior.)

9. What is your role in the conflict? Do you provoke? Do you ignore his or her positives? What alternative adaptive behavior could you use in the future? (It is not always a matter of who started it, but rather how things can be improved. Are there any changes in your behavior that could improve the

situation? Why not ask your partner what you can do to make it better?)

    10. You may think that what has happened is awful. (Try putting things in perspective. Think about what happened along a continuum—what could be worse? Are you looking at things out of proportion to what they are?)

    Each partner may be given cognitive homework through which he collects examples of his thoughts and attempts some of the challenges already indicated. As the therapist proceeds, certain themes emerge for each partner. These are referred to as cognitive schemata or schemas, the predispositions of how each partner views interactions according to specific issues. These individual schemas involve themes such as control, abandonment, humiliation, inadequacy, manipulation, rejection, validation, and a variety of other content areas.

    Table 9–4 lists some examples of specific content areas for different interpersonal schemas that affect marital conflict. There is no real limitation on the number of schemas we could generate. These examples illustrate some predispositions in the way individuals might perceive interactions and their vulnerability to these particular schemas.

    For one couple, the husband's schema was a fear of being controlled and the wife's schema was a need to be validated. Whenever the wife would express strong negative feelings ("You don't listen to me"), the husband would become anxious and angry because he perceived her need to be validated as an attempt to control him. Consequently he withdrew from these interactions, further exacerbating her need to be validated and confirming her suspicion that he was not interested in her feelings. With another couple, the wife, who had suffered from a long-standing depression, would also express her negative feelings about work. From her perspective, she wanted validation that her situation was difficult to cope with. The husband's schema was one of excessive responsibility: when she de-

Table 9–4. Examples of Interpersonal Schemas in Marital Conflict

Schema	Examples
Abandonment	My partner will leave me. I cannot function or I cannot be happy without my partner.
Autonomy/Control	My partner is trying to control me. I must be in control.
Demanding standards	Our relationship should be wonderful all the time.
Entitlement	I should get my way. My partner should meet my needs. I shouldn't have to work at a relationship.
Validation	My partner should see things my way. I need to express all my feelings.
Rejection	If I assert myself, my partner will reject me. I can't stand rejection.
Punitiveness	Either my partner will punish me or I must punish my partner.
Engulfment	If I let my partner get too close, I will lose my identity.
Excessive responsibility	Either I am responsible for my partner's needs or he is responsible for my needs.
Self-sacrifice	In order for me to be a good person, I need to put my partner's needs before my own.
Dramatic display	A good relationship must be filled with intense emotion.

scribed her problem, he immediately believed that he was responsible for solving her problem. This activated his belief that he was not adequate to solve her problem, resulting in his angry thought, "She's presenting me with an impossible problem to solve." For both of these couples, it was helpful to indicate to the husband that the wife was not attempting to control or place responsibility on the husband. Rather, the husband could become more effective by practicing active listening skills, such as inquiry, validation, and empathy.

CONCLUDING COMMENTS

Two out of three couples show improvement in cognitive therapy. Following the recommendations outlined in this chapter, premarital counseling is predictive of whether couples remain together two to three years after marriage (Markman 1994). As indicated at the beginning of this chapter, marital therapy not only alleviates the individual's depression, but also improves the quality of the relationship. Therapists differ as to their belief in the desirability of supplementing couples therapy with individual sessions. We have found it to be immensely useful to use individual meetings, especially in the initial evaluation stage. Partners in the privacy of individual sessions are far more willing to identify past or current affairs that may interfere with the pursuit of joint therapy. I make it a rule for patients to forego any extramarital relationships while they are pursuing conjoint therapy. The rationale is that each partner must be willing to devote as much commitment as possible to improving this relationship. Furthermore, if the therapist knows about a current extramarital relationship but hides this information from the other partner, he enters into a collusive, unethical deception. By clarifying the nature of the therapeutic contract—one based on honesty and commitment—the therapist provides a role model for an effective relationship.

Finally, there may be some patients who are not ready for marital therapy. Individuals who are currently abusing substances or those with severe personality disorders, such as paranoid or borderline personalities, may need intense individual treatment before they can hope to benefit from conjoint therapy. The therapist should not hesitate to require this individual treatment prior to pursuing conjoint therapy.

10

CASE
CONCEPTUALIZATION

A frequent criticism of cognitive therapy is that it appears too technique-oriented, too focused on a non-theoretical, or non-conceptual approach to the individual patient. Early on, Beck (1976) warned against the trial-and-error approach of technique-oriented cognitive therapy, urging the clinician to develop a treatment plan and conceptualization. Persons (1989) has encouraged cognitive therapists to guide their therapy by case conceptualization rather than a shotgun approach of techniques.

I will now attempt to illustrate how the cognitive therapist utilizes case conceptualization in working with the patient. I will outline developmental and cognitive issues that are often important in addressing the patient's problems.

DEVELOPMENTAL ISSUES

According to Bowlby (1969, 1973, 1980), schemas about self and other are often established in early childhood as object representations. He has convincingly argued that the infant is innately predisposed to form a focused attachment and that impediments to this attachment lead to the development of schemas or cognitive representations of future attachment. For example, the infant or young child may develop a secure attachment, an anxious attachment, or an ambivalent attachment (one that vacillates among anger, anxiety, and detachment). These early attachment schemas operate on a level of unawareness for the individual, but determine further information processing.

A second developmental factor is that early schemas are formed at a preoperational level of intelligence (Piaget 1954, 1970), marked by egocentrism, centration, magical thinking, and moral realism. These structural limitations of preoperational intelligence are also characteristic of the thinking of many depressives (Leahy 1985, 1991, 1995).

Egocentrism refers to the tendency of the young child to see things only from his perspective. In the case of negative schemas, it is implied that the self is the cause of negative events. Centration refers to the fact that the individual focuses on one dimension—usually something that is immediately present and salient. Centration results in the inability to recognize variation of self and others across time and situations, resulting in a tendency in the depressive to overgeneralize negatives beyond the immediate situation. Magical thinking, characteristic of the moral reasoning of the preoperational child, is reflected in the tendency of depressives to use their emotions as a guide to reality, to engage in mind reading, and to believe they are the cause of events only tangentially related to them. Finally, moral realism involves the tendency to believe that bad things happen to bad people and that a negative personal action cannot be mitigated by extenuating circumstances. Thus, the structurally limited depressive believes that his depression is proof that he is bad and that there are no factors that could mitigate his guilt.

Compensation and Avoidance

Bowlby (1980) has proposed that the child or adult attempts to adapt to early maladaptive schemas either by compensating for the supposed personal deficits or by avoiding situations in which the personal deficit might be manifested. Similar to Adler's (1964) theory of social power, Bowlby claims that the child with a sense of personal inferiority may attempt to overcome this schema by trying to achieve great things. The short person, whose height is viewed as a deficiency, may attempt to become more aggressive than others. The underlying assumption is, "If I can be tougher than others, they won't see my real weakness."

Similarly, one might avoid the schema by not confronting situations where the schema might be activated. The child who has been rejected by his mother may avoid interactions with women lest he be rejected again. The underlying belief is "Why bother to approach women? They'll only reject me." Another method of avoidance is not to think about anything related to the schema or to distract one's attention from the schema.

The difficulty that ensues from the strategies of compensation and avoidance is that the schema is never directly examined. The individual is too busy trying to compensate and avoid to directly examine the early maladaptive schema "I am helpless." The cognitive therapist, in developing a case conceptualization and in interpreting life events for patients, may find it useful to ask the following questions about these schemas:

How did your parents (siblings, peers, teachers) teach you that
   you are helpless?
When you learned the schema, you were 5 years old. Do you
   think it is wise to guide your life by what a 5-year-old thinks?
What evidence is there that you are not helpless? Or that you
   are helpless?
How would you rate yourself on a continuum from 0 percent to
   100 percent competent? Helpless?
Is it necessary to be invulnerable or perfect to prove you are
   not helpless?
What is the consequence of demanding this of yourself?
Is it ever OK to be helpless? To fail? To depend on others? To
   be disapproved of?
How would you challenge your mother and father, now that
   you are an adult, if they were to describe you as helpless?

In the case study described below, the foregoing questions
were posed to someone who attempted to be invulnerable in
order to overcome his fundamental fear that he was helpless.

Case Study

Presenting problem

Bill was a 30-year-old single male with obsessive-compulsive and
narcissistic features. For two years he had been running his own
small company, and he came to therapy complaining of depression and anxiety for the previous three years, during which time
he had lost almost thirty pounds. He suffered from severe insomnia during those years, sleeping only three to four hours a
night. Bill felt trapped in a relationship with a girlfriend who made
excessive financial demands on him and disparaged his ability to

succeed. Bill felt financially responsible for his girlfriend, his father, and his two adult brothers.

He kept three telephones in bed with him in case a family member needed him or in case there was a business deal from Japan in the middle of the night. Concerned about his weight, he would compulsively weigh himself several times a day. Bill worried constantly about going bankrupt or letting other people down. He was highly obsessed that he had an undiagnosed illness that caused his weight loss and fatigue, and worried that if he had to go to a hospital he would be infected with AIDS. His history revealed no high-risk behavior and he had tested HIV-negative twice during the prior two years.

Developmental history

Bill grew up in a highly visible family: his father had been a successful Wall Street investor and his mother was well known in the community. His idealization of his childhood was evident when he came to a therapy session with a framed photograph of the family estate—a home he said he would like to own again. The estate had been lost when his father declared bankruptcy. (The narcissistic father would require Bill, at the age of 10, to read the *New York Times* every day and provide him with a summary. The difficulty was even greater for him since he was dyslexic.)

Bill recalled that his mother's manic-depressive illness caused her to use him for target practice by firing her gun in his direction, or else threatening suicide. When Bill was 14 his mother left her husband and home, taking the three sons with her and staying in cheap motels as she made her way south. Two years later Bill had saved enough money from his business schemes to run away from mother, assist in the escape of his two brothers for whom he felt personally responsible, and return to his father.

Bill attended college, but due to his dyslexia and a shortage of funds, he never graduated. Nevertheless, he managed to obtain a good job in an investment house and to accumulate considerable financial resources, which he later invested in his own company.

Bill was filled with grandiose ideas of his future wealth, fame, and power.

Although Bill was shorter than most men, he had become a skilled master of karate and aikido. He described his confidence and excitement in placing himself in dangerous situations, hoping someone would attack him so he could demonstrate his invulnerability. He described his excitement when he spent time in Eastern Europe during the collapse of communism and witnessed open gunfights in the street. He also enjoyed driving his sports car at excessive speeds, tempting death.

Schemas and Scripts

I have distinguished schemas from scripts (Leahy 1991, 1992a, 1995). Schemas are similar to concepts that direct information processing and result in selective attention to or memory for information relevant to the schema. Consequently, if the individual believes he is inferior, he will focus on information related to his failures and discount information related to his successes. In Bill's case, his schemas of physical vulnerability (derived from his mother's threats on his life) led him to focus on danger to himself. He compensated for this schema by developing talents in the martial arts.

Scripts, on the other hand, refer to the patient's interpersonal world so that he constructs a world that allows him to compensate for or avoid his underlying schema. The schema "I'm weak," might result in a script in which the patient compensates for his fear of weakness by attempting to become invulnerable. Conversely, the patient may avoid his schema of weakness by refusing to take on any challenges.

Consider the following schemas and scripts (or compensations) evident in Bill's history:

Schema: "I am weak and vulnerable physically."

Scripts of compensation: Bill becomes proficient in the martial arts, places himself in dangerous situations, demonstrates counterphobic behavior. He is compulsive about checking his weight and health, hypervigilant about any physical problem.

Schema: "I am inferior."

Scripts of compensation: Bill compulsively achieves, displaying his wealth, living beyond his means at times, socializing with the rich and famous. He surrounds himself with people who depend on him; that is, his father works for him and his brothers need his financial support. He tries to prove to his girlfriend that he can provide her with the lavish lifestyle she wants.

Schema: "I will be abandoned."

Scripts of compensation and avoidance: Bill insists that others need him and that he will take care of them financially. If they need him, they won't leave him. Furthermore, some friends who have befriended him for his investment savvy could not truly abandon him because he knows he could never become attached to them.

Developmental Analysis

After the initial intake evaluation was completed, the therapist provided Bill with a case conceptualization based on Bowlby's attachment theory and Beck's cognitive model. First, it was indicated to Bill that threats of, and actual abandonment during childhood led to his compulsive caretaking of others. This was based on two underlying assumptions: "If I take care of others, they will never leave me" and "If I focus on others' needs, I do not have to think about my own needs for attachment."

Second, Bill's exposure to physical danger from his mother led to an attempt to prove that he was physically invulnerable, a fear he compensated for by acquiring skills in karate and exposing himself to danger. However, because of his underlying belief that he was really physically vulnerable, he had become hypervigilant about his health—interpreting every malady as evidence of a fatal and uncontrollable disease.

Third, the association in his mind between his father's business failures and the disintegration of his family led to three beliefs: first, he idealized the lost Eden of his family—a narcissistic idealization that provided him with a goal of returning to an ideal and secure state; second, he believed that financial success was the only means to any interpersonal security, placing further pressure on himself to perform; and, third, he had chosen a girlfriend who was a mother-surrogate to whom he was trying to prove, unlike his father, that he was worthy of her love.

Because his attempts to compensate for his underlying schemas of vulnerability, inferiority, and abandonment could never be sufficient (he could never become totally invulnerable, more successful than everyone else, or completely sure of anyone's fidelity), he would always be at the mercy of these early schemas and scripts. The goal of therapy was to help him understand these connections and to learn that one can acknowledge attachment needs, vulnerability, and fear. Moreover, one could place limits on the needs of family members and still pursue a productive life.

BEHAVIORAL INTERVENTIONS

Although the developmental analysis was shared with Bill early in therapy, the first interventions were behavioral. The reason for this choice was that we wished to eliminate his most troublesome obsessive-compulsive symptoms first and to establish the credibility of the therapy so that more challenging and disturbing issues could then be addressed.

In order to reduce Bill's insomnia he was instructed in appropriate sleep hygiene or behavioral rules for sleeping. Each night Bill recorded the time he went to bed, how long he thought it took him to fall asleep, the frequency of waking during the night, and the time that he finally arose. He was given the following rules:

> The bed is for sleep or sex only. Do not lie in bed reading, watching TV, or talking on the phone. Reduce liquid intake after 7 P.M.. Avoid caffeinated beverages and foods. Do not exercise in the evening, since this will only increase your arousal. Try to go to bed and get up at the same times each night and morning. Avoid naps during the day. If you are lying awake and do not fall asleep, get out of bed, go into another room, and perform a boring task for fifteen minutes. Do not try to fall asleep, since this will only increase your frustration. Rather, try to practice giving up or surrendering—as if you were abandoning the idea of sleep. Challenge your thoughts: "I'll never get to sleep" or "I'll be too tired to function." Give yourself time to develop better sleep habits.

Bill was asked to remove all phones from the bedroom and place them on answering machines. Friends and family were instructed never to call him after 10 P.M. Within one month, Bill was getting over six hours of sleep a night.

The next behavioral interventions were focused on Bill's compulsive hypochondriacal weight checking. He was told to delay checking weight as long as possible and eventually not to check his weight for several weeks. He was told to eat even if he was not hungry in order to build up an appetite. These initial interventions were extremely effective and produced long-lasting improvements in sleep habits and weight gain.

COGNITIVE ANALYSIS

Bill's maladaptive early schemas were supported by a variety of automatic thought distortions:

Fortune telling: I will go bankrupt. My girlfriend will leave me.

Catastrophizing: My weight loss means I'm dying. I'll get AIDS.

Personalizing: I have to take care of my brothers. If the relationship with my girlfriend doesn't work out, it must be my fault.

Mind reading: People can see I'm anxious.

Labeling: I must have an incurable disease.

Discounting positives: My past success doesn't mean anything unless I continue to succeed.

Dichotomous thinking: Either I'm a complete success or a complete failure.

In addition to these automatic thought distortions, Bill had a variety of maladaptive and demanding assumptions related to his schemas of vulnerability, abandonment, and inferiority:

"I have to be completely sure of my invulnerability or I will be in danger."

"I can never let my guard down. I can never relax. I'll lose my edge."

"People only like me for my wealth and influence. Without that, they would reject me."

"I can never depend on anyone. I have to get people to depend on me."

We examined all of these automatic thoughts and assumptions by evaluating the costs and benefits of each thought, evidence for and against the thought, the double standard technique ("Would you apply these same standards to others? Why not?"), and acting against the thought. In examining Bill's fear of vulnerability and helplessness, I asked him to imagine himself in a crib at night in a dark room, small and helpless, infantile. He grew increasingly anxious. I asked him to tell me his thoughts:

Bill: I feel very angry. Like I want to kill you.
Therapist: What about this image disturbs you?
Bill: Either I'll be killed or I'll kill someone.
Therapist: How do you relate this to your memory of your mother shooting at you?
Bill: I thought I was going to be killed. And then I vowed that my brothers and I would never be in that position again.
Therapist: You mean the position of being helpless?
Bill: That's right. I never want to be helpless again.

Part of the cognitive analysis was an evaluation of how Bill's interactive reality—his choices of girlfriend, other friends, and his sense of obligation to his family—was related to these early schemas. For example, his choice of a cold, rejecting, judgmental girlfriend who questioned his ability to support her lifestyle was an attempt to relive successfully his father's experience with his mother, who left when his father failed financially.

We developed a "Bill of Rights" for him and focused on his right to set limitations and not be responsible for his brothers and his girlfriend. As he became more assertive in setting limits, they challenged him, telling him he was becoming too selfish and that he was losing his edge. He began feeling better, eventually broke up with the girlfriend, and developed a relationship with another woman whom he eventually married.

TRANSFERENCE

Bill's schemas played themselves out in the transference. One strategy he used was to idealize the therapist as the perfect rescuer so that he could feel secure. A second strategy was to try to convince the therapist that, in fact, he *could* live up to his ideal goals of wealth and power. A third strategy was to attempt to buy the therapist or, rather, to test the therapist's values. Toward the completion of therapy, Bill said that he wanted to thank me for all I had done and offered to buy me a Ferrari. When I told him that my fee was sufficient compensation, he remarked, "I was really trying to test you."

OUTCOME

After eight months of therapy, Bill's sleep patterns were normal; he had regained all of his lost weight, and he had broken off with the narcissistic girlfriend and begun a relationship with another woman. When he told her of his concerns that his business might fail and he might not be able to support her, she reminded him that she was a physician and could support both of them. Bill was successful in setting limits for his two brothers, who attempted to induce guilt in him for not taking care of them. He was no longer obsessively preoccupied with financial success although he still enjoyed it, and he was able to acknowledge his own concerns to his fiancée. An attempt to reestablish contact with his mother was a bitter disappointment, but it allowed him to recognize that she no longer controlled or threatened him. Two years after the completion of therapy, I received a card from Bill and his wife announcing the birth of their child. Bill indicated that he had achieved some sense of satisfaction and perspective in his life.

SUMMARY

The case conceptualization of Bill's symptoms allowed both the therapist and the patient to piece together a rather complicated and chronic pattern of maladaptive behaviors, anxiety, and depression. Because Bill was highly invested in compensating and avoiding his early schemas, his resistance to change could be addressed by providing him with a developmental analysis of his problems. This case illustrates how the cognitive therapist can integrate behavioral techniques in dealing with insomnia and obsessive-compulsive disorder with cognitive techniques to help him identify and challenge a client's automatic thoughts, maladaptive assumptions, and underlying schemas. The developmental analysis helped the patient understand why he was so emotionally committed to a pattern of behaving, thinking, and relating that appeared irrational and self-destructive but nevertheless had considerable appeal for him.

11

RESISTANCE AND COUNTERTRANSFERENCE

The novice at cognitive therapy may be struck by the optimism and active nature of the therapist. The therapist who attends workshops on cognitive therapy may come away believing that cognitive therapy is a panacea. The pressure of managed care to reduce therapy to a minimum number of sessions may also encourage us to believe that cognitive therapy can work miracles. However, as effective and proactive as it is, cognitive therapy is not a panacea. Patients resist treatment and therapists manifest their countertransference.

RESISTANCE

Consider the following example. A single female patient, Susan, is a lawyer who complains of loneliness and her inability to meet men. She lives at home with her parents and two sisters. When she was a child, her father was verbally and physically abusive. She had been in therapy with other therapists for seven years and had previously taken antidepressant medication. She is still depressed and forlorn about her loneliness. Her previous therapist encouraged her to be more outgoing, but this had little effect. She is an attractive, intelligent, personable woman who enjoys ballroom dancing. What has kept her from improving?

1. Examining motivation to change. Therapist and patient often agree on the surface that the patient really wants to change. However, change incurs risk—improvement may lead to the possibility of more serious, more public failure. The therapist and patient explore the costs and benefits of dating more men.

Therapist: What would some of the benefits be if you dated?

Susan: I would feel more normal. Maybe I could find someone to have a good relationship with.

Therapist: What are some of the disadvantages of dating more?

Susan: I might find out that I can't do it. Maybe no one would want me. I'd be rejected.

Therapist: What would be the disadvantage of having a more intimate relationship with a man?

Susan: I might be humiliated.

Therapist: How would that happen?

Susan: He might find out that I'm not experienced. He might ridicule me.

Therapist: Is there any other disadvantage to intimacy?

Susan: He would have power over me. I'd be helpless.

Therapist: How would he have power over you?

Susan: He would be more experienced than I, so he would be in charge.

Therapist: Are there any other disadvantages?

Susan: Well, if I met someone and I moved out, I'd be deserting my family.

2. Examining reasons to resist. Clearly, Susan had many more reasons not to change. She believed that she would not be able to date, and since she'd had only two dates in her life, her past experience would seem to support her pessimism.

Therapist: What are some of the positive qualities you could offer?

Susan: I don't know if I have any.

Therapist: Well, let me ask you what you would like in a partner. What qualities would you want him to have?

Susan: I'd want him to have good values. Smart, a good listener, someone who would not impose himself on me. Attractive, but not conceited. Someone who would want a more equal relationship. Someone who is understanding.

Therapist: OK. Do you have any of these qualities? For example, do you have good values, are you smart, are you a good listener?

Susan: I guess I have all of these qualities.

Therapist: Then you're looking for someone who has your qualities?

Susan: Yes.

Therapist: How do you reconcile that with the idea that you have little to offer in a relationship?

Susan: I see what you're getting at. But I don't have any sexual experience.

Therapist: Do you think a man would reject you for that reason?

Susan: Maybe.

Therapist: And maybe not?

Susan's core belief was that a man would have power over her and would ridicule her if she became intimate. I decided to explore this as an assertion issue.

Therapist: How would he have power over you?

Susan: He would have more experience.

Therapist: But how does that give him power?

Susan: He would know more. He would be in a position of teaching me.

Therapist: What if you found that you disliked what he said or did? What could you do?

Susan: I could tell him.

Therapist: And what if he wouldn't listen?

Susan: I could break up with him.

Therapist: So doesn't that mean you have power? You could assert yourself.

Susan: That's true. I could.

Susan's other reason to resist was based on loyalty to her family. Her younger sister was developmentally disabled and Susan felt an obligation to take care of her. However, both her parents and her other sister lived at home.

Therapist: Why is it your responsibility to stay at home and take care of everyone?

Susan: Because they need my help.

Therapist: What would happen if you moved out?

Susan: I guess my parents would be able to take care of my sister. But Mother needs my support.

Therapist: What does your mother need from you?

Susan: She needs to talk with me.

Therapist: Can she do that on the phone?

Susan: Yes.

Therapist: When you moved out five years ago for a few months, did anything bad happen to the family?

Susan: No.

Therapist: So what would really happen if you moved out?

Susan: Probably nothing.

Therapist: Is there an advantage for you to believe that your family needs you to stay at home?

Susan: I guess then I don't have to deal with my own problems.

3. *Providing a plan.* Susan believed she didn't know how to meet men.

Therapist: When you are at a dance and a man starts a conversation, what goes through your mind?

Susan: He'll find out I'm not interesting.

Therapist: What do you do?

Susan: Sometimes I just don't say anything. Sometimes I'll excuse myself and go to the bathroom.

Therapist: So you predict you'll be rejected and you withdraw?

Susan: Yes.

Therapist: What's the consequence of that?

Susan: I guess I never give it a chance.

I decided to give Susan a plan. Since she was always looking for any sign of rejection, I decided to turn her into a positive tracker who would focus on any evidence that a man was interested in her. We made up a list of behaviors that would show a man's interest—for example, looking at her, talking to her, touching her, complimenting her, smiling, and asking her to dance. Her assignment was to go to the next dance and collect all the information she could that showed someone's interest. Furthermore, I asked her to try to prolong her interactions with men by asking them questions about themselves. Much to her surprise over the next two weeks, she found there was considerable interest in her and when she prolonged her interactions with men, they were interested in knowing more about her.

4. *Challenging negative thoughts.* We agreed to examine whatever negative thoughts Susan had about meeting men

and developing relationships. Susan was asked to record any negative thoughts that she had about meeting men and dating them. These were:

If I talk to someone, he won't be interested.
I'll be rejected.
No one would want me.
I have nothing to offer.
I'm too old to meet someone.
I have a fatal flaw. I'm inexperienced.
I'll be rejected if a man finds out I'm inexperienced.
Men will humiliate me and dominate me.
If I date someone, I'm obligated to continue dating him. I'm
    trapped.

We decided to examine each of these automatic thoughts by looking at the costs and benefits of the thought, evidence for and against the thought, the implication (vertical descent), double-standard technique, and setting up behavioral experiments to test the thought. We considered the thought "I'll be rejected."

Costs/Benefits

Costs: If I believe this, then I won't approach anyone and I'll
    never have a relationship. I'll feel helpless and alone.
Benefits: I won't put myself in the position of being rejected. I
    won't look foolish.

Susan concluded that the costs of believing that she would be rejected outweighed the benefits. We next examined the costs and benefits of taking risks and putting herself in a position to be rejected. Here the benefits outweighed the costs; by taking more risks she increased her chances of meeting someone.

Evidence

For: I don't have anyone now. There must be something wrong with me.

Against: I haven't been rejected before. I'm attractive and nice and men might like me. I've been the one doing the rejecting.

Susan concluded that there was no strong evidence that she would be rejected and she realized that she was cutting her losses before they occurred by withdrawing from interactions with men to whom she was attracted.

What Would Be So Bad About Being Rejected?

If I were rejected, it would mean there's something wrong with me.

——> If there's something wrong with me, then no one would want me.

——> Then I would always be alone.

We examined each of these implications. For example, someone might not like you because he has different taste. Maybe he likes blondes rather than brunettes. We also looked at the double-standard: "If you don't find a man attractive, does that mean no woman on earth would find him attractive?" "Do you have to be attractive to every man in the world to be attractive enough to date?" "Are there any women or men who have problems and who do form relationships?" "Is everyone who is married a perfect person?" "What would you still be able to do even if a man did not show an interest in you?"

In order to further decrease the emphasis on rejection, we decided to set collecting experience interacting with and dating men as a therapeutic goal. The purpose of this assignment was to decatastrophize rejection and help her gain experience in rewarding and being rewarded by men.

Are You Idealizing Other People?

As with many single people with little experience in intimacy, there is a tendency to idealize or mystify the opposite sex. We examined this mystification with Susan.

Therapist: Do you think that men and women are very different?

Susan: Yes. Men are confident and strong. They're in charge. Women tend to be dependent on men. I don't want to be dependent.

Therapist: When a man goes to a party or a dance, what kinds of things do you think he feels insecure about?

Susan: I've never thought of that. I guess he wonders if he'll be able to meet a woman.

Therapist: When he sees a woman standing there, what kinds of insecure thoughts does he have?

Susan: He's probably wondering whether she'll find him interesting—whether she'll reject him.

Therapist: That sounds like some of your concerns.

Susan: Yes.

Therapist: So if a man thought that you were encouraging him—if you looked at him and smiled—do you think he would be more likely to approach you?

Susan: I guess he would.

Therapist: Do you think that in the past you inadvertently made it hard for men because you did not reinforce them?

Susan: Yes, that's true.

Therapist: If you thought of men having a lot of insecurities, a lot of fears just like yours of being rejected, you might take the initiative and make it easy for them.

Susan: I guess I never thought that men were so insecure.

Therapist: You don't know the men that I know.

Susan: (laughs) That's probably true.

Evaluate the Double Standard

Quite often, resistant patients find it easier to challenge their negative thoughts when they try to apply them to other people. In this case, we examined the negative thought "If a man is not interested in a woman it means that the woman is defective and no one will ever want her."

Therapist: If you saw a woman talking with a man and the man walked away, what would you think?

Susan: I'd think he was rude.

Therapist: What if a woman friend of yours dated a guy and after a couple of months the guy said, "It's not working out for me. I think we should stop seeing each other"? Would you think that she would never be able to have another relationship?

Susan: No. It just didn't work out for them. It could work out with someone else.

Therapist: What is your rationale for being easier on other women than you are on yourself? Why don't you conclude that they are defective, but you think that you are?

Susan: I can't think of any good reason for that.

Therapist: It sounds like you have a double standard—a higher standard for yourself than for others. Does that seem fair?

Susan: Now that you put it that way, I guess it's not fair to me.

Another useful technique is to have the patient role-play her negative thoughts against someone else with the same problem. In this case, I played the role of a man who was rejected by a woman at a dance. I asked Susan to judge me negatively and tell me that I would never be able to meet anyone else.

Therapist (role-playing): I went up to that woman, Betsy, and she didn't seem to want to talk with me.

Susan (role-playing negative thoughts toward therapist): That must mean that she didn't like you. Probably that happens a lot to you.

Therapist: Do you think that I should approach other women?

Susan: Probably not. There must be something wrong with you that Betsy didn't want to talk with you.

Therapist: What could it be?

Susan: I don't know. You must have some fundamental flaw.

Therapist: But other women were interested in talking with me before.

Susan: They don't count. The only thing that counts is this one rejection.

During the role-play, Susan became uncomfortable and laughed. When we discussed this, she declared that she would never think this about someone else, and she could never imagine saying such cruel things to others. Consequently, we changed the rules of the next role-play so that Susan could be a supportive friend.

Therapist (role-playing): Betsy wasn't interested in talking with me.

Susan (role-playing supportive friend): There are lots of other women to talk to. Maybe she's not your type.

Therapist: But I really wanted to talk with her. She's attractive.

Susan: Haven't there been other women you've met before who liked you?

Therapist: Yeah, but they're not here right now.

Susan: I guess you'll have to be patient and keep approaching other women. There's no urgency to meet someone.

Therapist: I think that if Betsy doesn't want to talk with me, it must mean that I'm defective.

Susan: It doesn't mean anything about you. For one thing, she doesn't even know you, so how could she be any judge of who you are? Other people like you. You don't have to be liked by everyone, do you?

In the foregoing role-play, Susan began to feel more confident challenging her negative thoughts when they were being expressed by someone else. She found it easier to defend someone else than to defend herself. The double-standard technique is useful in that it allows the patient to step outside of his or her resistance to change and see how automatic thoughts do not make sense when applied to someone else.

Examine the Source of Negative Schemas

Susan's negative view of relationships was based almost entirely on her observations of her parents. Her father had been abusive when she was younger, but now she almost totally avoided him. We examined how she had set limits on her father and how he was not typical of other men. Susan had become quite capable of standing up to him. We also reviewed how she was different from her mother. Unlike her mother, Susan was self-supporting and could move away from home anytime that she wanted to. This was helpful in encouraging her in pursuing relationships with men.

One way of challenging the negative schema is to have the patient describe what her schemas would be if she grew up in a healthier family. What would her view of men be if she had a father who was respectful and rewarding? Another question to ask is why all other women do not have such negative schemas about men? What could account for these differences in the perception of men? This helps the patient recognize how she has overgeneralized a bad situation. By recognizing that her negative schema is due to an idiosyncratic personal history, she can realize that her schema is not reality but rather a particular way of looking at reality.

The early maladaptive schema may be challenged by what I call retrospective cognitive therapy (Leahy 1985, 1991, 1992a, 1995, Young 1990). In retrospective cognitive therapy we are schema-focused in that we attempt to identify the early experiences that gave rise to the schema and try to modify it. Susan was asked to recall a situation in which she felt humiliated by her father—the origin of her humiliation schema. She was asked to close her eyes, imagine being humiliated, and try to recall a scene from her past when her father had made her feel that way. The image that came to mind was when she was a teenager, and her father walked in on her while she was taking a shower. She felt that this was sexually inappropriate. She felt both frightened and angry. In her recollection, her father yelled at her because she protested his presence in the bathroom.

I asked Susan to keep this image vividly in her mind while she practiced repeating an angry, assertive response to her father.

Therapist: Susan, I want you to tell your father that he cannot be in the bathroom with you. Tell him so he knows you are powerful and strong and will not take any of his abuse.

Susan (role-playing toward father image): Get the hell out of here! You don't belong in here! I won't take your abuse any longer!

Therapist: Tell him why you don't like him.

Susan: You are an abusive bastard! You have abused all of us. You won't treat me like you've treated my mother! I want you out of my life!

We continued these retrospective role-plays with Susan asserting herself toward her father, imagining herself as physically larger and stronger than her father. These role-plays were disturbing but cathartic. They provided her with the opportunity to stand up to her father and feel victorious rather than humiliated. We next turned to the question of how she could make sure that no other man would ever treat her that way.

Therapist: What if another man in your life tried to abuse you or humiliate you?

Susan: I would tell him he can't do that to me. I won't take that from anyone!

Therapist: Well, if you won't take that from anyone, then you can protect yourself from being humiliated. You don't have to keep putting up boundaries with men if you can assert yourself.

Susan: That's right. Maybe I can be in control.

Therapist: What if you were involved with a guy and he made fun of your lack of sexual experience? What could you do?

Susan: I could walk out. I could tell him to go to hell.

Therapist: So ultimately you're in charge, aren't you?

Susan: I guess I am.

Set Up Behavioral Experiments

In order to challenge Susan's fear of rejection and her fear that she might be humiliated and dominated, we agreed to set goals for her to flirt whenever possible by looking at, smiling at, talking to, and reinforcing men. Furthermore, we role-played how she could be assertive on dates—that is, how she could set limits on sexual advances, how she could say no, how she could show an interest in seeing someone again. We also explored her deeper fear of sexual humiliation and we examined how she had the power to set limits on anyone she was with.

Susan proved to be a diligent and cooperative patient once we had examined and challenged her different sources of resistance. She would carry out most homework assignments, tape our sessions, and provide me with corrective feedback if something was not going well. Much to her surprise, men began asking her out on dates. She began dating and learned she could set limits on men without crushing their egos or feeling as if she were a terrible person. Her success in dating became so apparent that she would come to sessions and claim that she was almost exhausted from all the time she was spending on dates. Ironically, her sister became quite envious of her success and tried to use Susan as bait to meet other men. We examined how her sister's problems in meeting men were not Susan's obligation to solve, nor was her success a misfortune for her sister. We agreed that her sister was a free agent who could find her own therapist if she so chose.

COUNTERTRANSFERENCE

Just as the patient may resist change in therapy, the therapist manifests his or her own countertransference. When I give workshops on cognitive therapy I like to demonstrate the nature of automatic thoughts, assumptions, and schemas by posing the following problem:

"Imagine that you have been working with a depressed

patient for the past year and she is still depressed after all your efforts. Whenever you have suggested homework exercises, she has refused. You now have to present this case to an audience of professionals at the hospital. How do you feel and what do you think?"

This example helps the therapist learning cognitive therapy understand the nature of cognitive assessment. Consider the following response from a psychiatric resident:

Resident: I would be angry at her.
Therapist: I would be angry at her because I'm thinking . . .
Resident: She won't do what I want her to do.
Therapist: That gets me angry because it makes me think . . .
Resident: She's in control . . .
Therapist: And what would that make you think?
Resident: She's not being fair. I've tried to help her and she's not doing her part.
Therapist: And if she's not fair and she's in control, what would that make you think?
Resident: She'll take advantage of me. I'll be dominated.
Therapist: And then what would happen?
Resident: Then I won't do well in my work.
Therapist: Then what would happen?
Resident: Then I won't be able to make a living. I'll become financially dependent.
Therapist: What would it mean to you to become financially dependent?
Resident: I'd have to rely on someone else for support. I'd have no control. I don't know if I could count on someone else.

What is interesting in this exchange is that this therapist views the patient's behavior from the perspective of fairness, power struggles, domination, and the fear of her own dependence. Her schema seems to be that she needs to be in control or she will become dependent on someone who is unreliable. One might expect this therapist to get into struggles with defiant and resistant patients. Her typical automatic thoughts are the following:

Mind reading and personalizing: The patient is trying to defeat me.
Personalizing: The patient is trying to control me.
Should: The patient should be fair and cooperate with me.
Low frustration tolerance: I can't stand it if the patient doesn't cooperate.
Fortune telling: I will be dominated if I don't resist.

In this workshop I indicated that the patient had these problems prior to being in therapy. The resistance was the problem for the patient, a problem that the therapist might develop some curiosity about. We examined the costs and benefits of the therapist's assumption "The patient should be cooperative."

Costs: I'll get angry at the patient. Patients are often uncooperative. If I get angry at the patient she might drop out of treatment or become more resistant.
Benefits: If I believe that the patient should be cooperative, then I won't allow myself to be controlled by the patient. This assumption will also motivate me to encourage the patient's cooperation.

As we examined the costs and benefits of this assumption, the resident began to realize that her assumptions about fairness and cooperation were unrealistic and kept her from understanding more fully the patient's reasons for not cooperating. Furthermore, by demanding cooperation the therapist is resisting the patient's own resistance.

We examined an adaptive assumption: "It might be useful for me to develop curiosity about why a patient is uncooperative." The costs and benefits of this new assumption were as follows:

Costs: Maybe I won't push the patient hard enough to change.
Benefits: I'll get to understand the patient better. I can always control being curious, but I can't always control whether the patient changes. It's more realistic. The patient might appreciate my curiosity.

This new assumption was viewed as more desirable than the assumption demanding fairness and cooperation.

Another maladaptive assumption in the countertransference is perfectionism. The perfectionist therapist views the patient's resistance as a personal failure on his own part. Moreover, the perfectionist therapist might demand perfection from the patient. Consider the following response from a therapist-in-training who, in fact, is an excellent cognitive therapist:

RL: What would it mean to you if the patient is not getting better?
Therapist: It means that I didn't do everything I should have done.
RL: What would that mean to you if it were true?
Therapist: I'm not as good as I could be.
RL: What would happen if that were true?
Therapist: I won't be successful in this field. I'll be a failure.
RL: And what would that mean to you?
Therapist: I couldn't respect myself.

Imagine the pressure on this therapist where self-esteem is dependent on resistant patients improving. We then examined these perfectionist assumptions.

RL: Has this patient gotten better with other therapists?

Therapist: No.

RL: Why should you be able to cure patients no one else has cured?

Therapist: I expect more of myself. Maybe I could be better.

RL: Do you know any therapist who cures all of his patients?

Therapist: No.

RL: Do you think you should be better than all other therapists?

Therapist: No.

RL: Is there anything in your work that you could respect? Have you ever helped anyone?

Therapist: Oh, yes. I have lots of patients whom I've helped. I guess I'm just focusing on this one patient and not recognizing what I've done for the others.

RL: Since you may be doing this for many years, what would be the advantage of accepting your limitations as a therapist?

Therapist: I won't be so frustrated. I could take credit for what I do accomplish and try to learn from more difficult cases.

It is beyond the scope of this book to examine the variety of interesting manifestations of countertransference. But we can easily recognize our own automatic thoughts and assumptions in the following:

Labeling: This patient is impossible. I'm not a good therapist.

Personalizing: Why is he doing this to me? He's out to defeat me.

Fortune telling: He'll never get better. Word will spread that I'm not a good therapist.

Awfulizing: I can't stand it when patients get angry at me and resist.

Shoulds: Patients shouldn't resist. They should be rational. They should cooperate. I should be able to cure this patient.

All-or-nothing thinking: Nothing has improved in this patient. He's still depressed.

Discounting the positives: Those other patients I helped were easy.

The reader might find it useful to identify his or her automatic thoughts, assumptions, and schemas about patients. You might identify a patient with whom you are having a particularly difficult time and list your feelings and automatic thoughts. Are you feeling angry, anxious, self-critical, bored, or defeated? Are you labeling, fortune telling, shoulding, or personalizing? Do you have personal schemas of unrelenting demanding standards (perfectionism), approval ("The patient should like me and appreciate my efforts."), or grandiosity ("I'm terrific and everyone should recognize that, including my patients!"). After you have identified your automatic thoughts ask yourself the following:

What are the costs and benefits of these beliefs?

What is the evidence for and against my belief?

Do I have a selective filter? A double standard? Am I viewing things out of perspective?

Would it be so bad if my thought were true?

How could I act against my negative thoughts about this patient?

Am I blaming the patient for her problems?

What would be the costs and benefits in developing curiosity about the patient's resistance and sharing that with him?

Do I view myself as a therapist or as a savior who is omnipotent? What are the advantages of accepting my limitations?

Am I using all the resources available to me? Perhaps I could reexamine my diagnosis and conceptualization. Perhaps medication needs to be changed. Perhaps I can consult with others about how to help this patient (and myself).

The foregoing questions are useful for all of us on a regular basis. As therapists we should always remind ourselves that we are only human, and we respond to frustration and attack with human thoughts and feelings. However, it is to no one's advantage if we act out on those thoughts or reject patients who are resistant. Therapy becomes a more meaningful learning and helping relationship when we are able to examine our own countertransference and use the same techniques on ourselves that we wish the patient to use. Perhaps by recognizing our own resistance to change—our countertransference—we can better place ourselves in the patient's perspective and more adequately empathize with the patient. It has been my experience that trainees in cognitive therapy who have been or are in therapy of almost any kind are better able to understand how the patient experiences therapy. None of us is free of countertransference, but the ability to examine one's own thoughts and feelings, and the willingness to modify them, is the mark of a therapist with depth. Cognitive therapy is not reducible to a cookbook of techniques, for it requires a continual examination of the relationship between patient and therapist. As Irvin Yalom (1989) indicates in *Love's Executioner,* we are all patients.

12

CONCLUSIONS

I began this book with the observation that the world of clinical psychology is changing. Patients are now informed consumers. They want to know what the treatment plan is, what rationale guides treatment, and how effective the treatment will be. The typical patient we see in private practice or in hospital settings expects greater initiative and feedback from the therapist. Indeed, economic factors in the marketplace of managed care may require many therapists to develop skills to justify their treatments to third-party payers. The demand for short-term, effective treatment is everywhere.

Cognitive therapy is not a panacea, nor is it the equivalent of "snap-out-of-it" therapy. Although I recognize that many patients may require long-term care—and many may prefer long-term care—the treatment of depression, generalized anxiety, social phobia, panic, agoraphobia, obsessive-compulsive disorder, and marital conflict may be addressed in a shorter-term modality. It is not uncommon for patients presenting with severe depression or anxiety to find relief from these symptoms within fifteen weeks. Many patients benefit from initial scheduling of two sessions per week, but many others can come only once a week. We seldom find it necessary to schedule patients more than twice each week, unless there is a serious psychiatric emergency, dissociative disorder, or such a severe personality disorder that the treatment requires more frequent therapy.

One of the reasons cognitive therapy can work in a shorter time frame with less frequent sessions is that the patient carries out much of the therapy through homework assignments. Furthermore, the therapist conveys a considerable amount of useful information that the patient can use in identifying and challenging negative thoughts. The patient does not have to go through the process of working through in order to get over depression or OCD. Rather, she can acquire new skills to solve the problems she confronts by using the therapy as a context in which the new skills were learned.

The underlying philosophy of the cognitive therapist is for the patient to become his own therapist. As you have learned from the suggestions in this book, the therapist encourages the patient to learn as much about his problem as possible and to actively generalize the techniques he learns in sessions to his experience outside of therapy. Some patients report they understand the techniques of therapy better when they think of how they would use them with friends. One patient who had difficulty getting some distance from her own thoughts found herself quite effective helping a friend look at the evidence for and against the friend's negative thoughts.

As I have indicated a number of times, the cognitive therapist uses bibliotherapy as part of the treatment. There are many excellent self-help books available from this perspective. We require all patients at our institute to read David

Burns's *The Feeling Good Handbook*, but we also encourage patients with specific problems to read other books and brochures that we make available to them. As someone who enjoys teaching in a medical school and university setting, I often think of patients as students in their therapy, learning about themselves in a non-judgmental context. This educative function is further enhanced by the skill acquisition components of cognitive therapy, such as learning how to communicate and listen better, and learning how to solve problems.

I encourage patients to tape-record sessions, because I find that patients can reinforce what they learn in this manner and can provide me with valuable feedback when I go astray or when something needs to be clarified. Taping is especially valuable with patients whose memory is impaired by depression. Some patients keep their tapes and review them months later when the same problems arise.

Because of the collaborative nature of cognitive therapy, where the patient is encouraged to view the therapy as a learning experience, issues of transference can be addressed with the patient in a direct and rational manner. The patient who believes the therapist does not understand or care about his problems may raise this issue in a direct way. The therapist will then employ all of the active listening skills we encourage couples to use, specifically inquiry, rephrasing, empathizing, and identifying. The therapist can then ask the patient to examine the thoughts that arise from these feelings of being misunderstood: "If you don't understand me right now, then you can't help me" or "No one cares about me." These hot cognitions in the session become material for further evaluation. Or the therapist may acknowledge that he does not understand the patient in the current context, and both therapist and patient can then examine ways in which understanding can be fostered.

Because of the active and rational approach used in cognitive therapy, we find that many patients can address their transference issues more readily. Some have criticized cognitive therapy as irrelevant to the transference, and, of course, there are many cognitive therapists (as well as other kinds of therapists) who do not handle transference well. However, I have found that the cognitive therapy approach can be readily adapted to the transference (or countertransference) and can help patient and therapist develop a more accurate case conceptualization and treatment plan.

We often get referrals from other therapists who believe that cognitive therapy may be helpful with limited problems—such as obsessive-compulsive symptoms or trichotillomania. Of course, the cognitive therapist can work in a symptom-focused manner and can work with the primary therapist whose orientation is somewhat different. However, it would be entirely inaccurate to claim that the cognitive approach cannot be used with patients whose problems are severe or complicated. There are excellent treatment approaches available for patients with chronic depression, personality disorders, eating disorders, and dissociative disorders—to name only a few. We have heard many patients who had spent years in other kinds of therapy comment that they learned much more about their chronic problems in a few weeks of cognitive therapy. Because therapy is based on the informed consumer approach and because the nature of cognitive inquiry is a central part of the treatment, many patients feel they can now put things together as never before. The therapist who is willing to pursue inquiry in depth—to keep asking, "And what would that mean to you?"—rather than jump down the patient's throat with rational responses will find himself and the patient amply rewarded with depth and complexity of material.

I wish to emphasize this point because novices in cognitive therapy can often trivialize the fascinating process of therapy by jumping to conclusions. I recall supervising a therapist who seemed to believe that cognitive therapy was equivalent to beating the patient in arguments and demonstrating to the patient how irrational he was. His rapid-fire comments and questions in role-plays began to irritate me and I told him so. I wanted him to know how it felt to have someone act like the Grand Inquisitor on Amphetamine.

And I wanted him to know that a cognitive therapist must be a caring and respectful person. Regardless of your orientation as a therapist, the capacity to show that you care about the patient is the first principle of all therapy. No matter how effective one thinks his or her therapeutic tools may be, few of us are willing to accept help from someone who does not care about us.

REFERENCES

Abramson, L. Y., Seligman, M. E. P., and Teasdale, J. D. (1978). Learned helplessness in humans: critique and reformulation. *Journal of Abnormal Psychology* 87: 102–109.

Adler, A. (1964). *Social Interest: A Challenge to Mankind.* Trans. J. Linton and R. Vaughan. New York: Capricorn Books.

Alford, B. A. (1986). Behavioral treatment of schizophrenic delusions: a single-case experimental analysis. *Behavior Therapy* 17: 637–644.

Alford, B. A., and Beck, A. T. (in press). *Cognitive Therapy: An Integration of Current Theory and Therapy.* New York: Guilford.

Alford, B. A., and Correia, C. J. (1994). Cognitive therapy of schizophrenia: theory and empirical status. *Behavior Therapy* 25: 17–33.

Alford, B. A., and Norcross, J. C. (1991). Cognitive therapy as integrative therapy. *Journal of Psychotherapy Integration* 1 (3): 175–190.

Alloy, L., and Abramson, L. Y. (1988). Depressive realism: four theoretical perspectives. In *Cognitive Processes in Depression,* ed. L. B. Alloy. New York: Guilford.

Bandura, A. (1969). *Principles of Behavior Modification.* New York: Holt, Rinehart, & Winston.

Barlow, D. (1988). *Anxiety and Its Disorders: The Nature and Treatment of Anxiety and Panic.* New York: Guilford.

Baucom, D. H. (1987). Attributions in distressed relations: How can we explain them? In *Heterosexual Relations, Marriage and Divorce,* ed. S. Duck and D. Perlman, pp. 177–206. London: Sage.

Baucom, D., and Epstein, N. (1990). *Cognitive-Behavioral Marital Therapy.* New York: Brunner/Mazel.

Beach, S. R. H., Sandeen, E. E., and O'Leary, K. D. (1992). *Depression in Marriage: A Model for Etiology and Treatment.* New York: Guilford.

Beck, A. T. (1967). *Depression: Causes and Treatment.* Philadelphia: University of Pennsylvania Press.

———— (1976). *Cognitive Therapy and the Emotional Disorders.* New York: International Universities Press.

———— (1987). Cognitive models of depression. *Journal of Cognitive Psychotherapy: An International Quarterly* 1 (1): 5–37.

———— (1988). *Love Is Never Enough.* New York: Harper & Row.

———— (In preparation). *Prisoners of Hate.*

Beck, A. T., Emery, G., and Greenberg, R. L. (1985). *Anxiety Disorders and Phobias: A Cognitive Perspective.* New York: Basic Books.

Beck, A. T., and Freeman, A. (1990). *Cognitive Therapy of Personality Disorders.* New York: Guilford.

Beck, A. T., Rush, A. J., Shaw, B. F., and Emery, G. (1979) . *Cognitive Therapy of Depression.* New York: Guilford.

Beck, A. T., Wright, F. D., Newman, C., and Liese, B. (1993). *Cognitive Therapy of Substance Abuse.* New York: Guilford.

Blatt, S. J., Quinlan, D. M., Chevron, E. S., et al. (1982). Dependency and self-criticism: psychological dimensions of depression. *Journal of Consulting and Clinical Psychology* 50: 113–124.

Bornstein, M. H. (1979). Perceptual Development: stability and change in feature perception. In *Psychological Development in Infancy,* ed. M. H. Bornstein and W. Kessen. Hillsdale, NJ: Lawrence Erlbaum.

Bowlby, J. (1969). *Attachment and Loss:* Vol. I. *Attachment.* New

York: Basic Books.

———— (1973). *Attachment and Loss:* Vol. II. *Separation: Anxiety and Anger.* New York: Basic Books.

———— (1980). *Attachment and Loss:* Vol. III. *Loss: Sadness and Depression.* London: Hogarth.

Burns, D. D. (1980). *Feeling Good: The New Mood Therapy.* New York: New American Library.

———— (1989). *The Feeling Good Handbook: Using the New Mood Therapy in Everyday Life.* New York: Morrow.

Buss, D. M. (1994). *The Evolution of Desire.* New York: Basic Books.

Chomsky, N. (1965). *Aspects of the Theory of Syntax.* Cambridge, MA: MIT Press.

———— (1968). *Language and Mind.* New York: Harcourt Brace.

Clark, D. M. (1986). A cognitive approach to panic. *Behavior Research and Therapy* 24: 461–470.

Clark, D., and Wells, A. (1995). A cognitive model of social phobia. In *Social Phobia: Diagnosis, Assessment, and Treatment,* ed. R. Heimberg, M. Liebowitz, D. Hope, and F. Schneier. New York: Guilford.

Cornford, F. M. (1957). *Plato's Theory of Knowledge.* New York: Bobbs-Merrill.

Datillio, F., and Padesky, C. (1990). *Cognitive Therapy with Couples.* Sarasota, FL: Professional Resource Exchange.

Derrida, J. (1973). *Speech and Phenomena.* Trans. D. B. Allison. Evanston, IL: Northwestern University Press.

DeRubeis, R. J., and Feeley, M. (1990). Determinants of change in cognitive therapy for depression. *Cognitive Therapy and Research* 14: 469–482.

Dodge, K. A., and Coie, J. D. (1987). Social information-processing factors in reactive and proactive aggression in children's peer groups. *Journal of Personality and Social Psychology,* 53: 1146–1158.

Donovan, D. M., and Marlatt, G. A., eds. (1988). *Assessment of Addictive Behaviors.* New York: Guilford.

Dweck, C., and Goetz, T. E. (1978). Attributions and learned helplessness. In *New Directions in Attribution Research,* vol. 2. ed. J. H. Harvey, W. J. Ickes, and R. F. Kidd. Hillsdale, NJ: Lawrence Erlbaum.

D'Zurilla, T. J. (1986). Problem-solving therapy: a social-competence approach to clinical intervention. New York: Springer.

Eibl-Eibesfeldt, I. (1970). *Ethology: The Biology of Behavior.* New York: Holt, Rinehart, and Winston.

Eidelson, J., and Epstein, N. (1982). Cognition and relationship maladjustment: development of a measure of dysfunctional relationship beliefs. *Journal of Consulting and Clinical Psychology* 50: 715–720.

Ellis, A. (1962). *Reason and Emotion in Psychotherapy.* New York: Lyle Stuart.

_____ (1976). Techniques of handling anger in marriage. *Journal of Marriage and Family Counseling* 2: 305–316.

_____ (1985). *Overcoming Resistance: Rational-Emotive Therapy with Difficult Clients.* New York: Springer.

Ellis, A., and Grieger, R., eds. (1977). *Handbook of Rational-Emotive Therapy.* New York: Springer.

Ferster, C. B., and Skinner, B. F. (1957). *Schedules of Reinforcement.* New York: New Appleton-Century-Crofts.

Fincham, F. D. (1985). Attribution processes in distressed and nondistressed couples: 2. Responsibility for marital problems. *Journal of Abnormal Psychology* 94: 183–190.

Foa, E., and Wilson, R. (1991). *Stop Obsessing: How to Overcome Your Obsessions and Compulsions.* New York: Bantam.

Furth, H. (1969). *Piaget and Knowledge: Theoretical Foundations.* New York: Prentice-Hall.

Gottman, J. (1995). *Why Marriages Succeed or Fail.* New York: Simon & Schuster.

Guerney, B. G. (1977). *Relationship Enhancement.* San Francisco: Jossey-Bass.

Guidano, V., and Liotti, G. (1983). *Cognitive Processes and the Emotional Disorders.* New York: Guilford.

Hamilton, M. (1960). A rating scale for depression. *Journal of Neurology, Neurosurgery, and Psychiatry.* 23: 56–62.

Hartmann, H. (1939/1958). *Ego Psychology and Problem of Adaptation.* New York: International Universities Press.

Heider, F. (1958). *The Psychology of Interpersonal Relations.* New York: Wiley.

Hope, D. A., and Heimberg, R. G. (1993). Social phobia and social anxiety. In *Clinical Handbook of Psychological Disorders: A Step-by-Step Treatment Manual,* ed. D. H. Barlow. New York: Guilford.

Horney, K. (1945). *Our Inner Conflicts: A Constructive Theory of*

Neurosis. New York: Norton.

_____ (1950). *Neurosis and Human Growth: The Struggle Toward Self-Realization.* New York: Norton.

Husserl, E. (1960). *Cartesian Meditation,* ed. D. Cairns. The Hague: Nijhoff.

Jacobson, N., and Margolin, G. (1980). *Marital Therapy: Strategies Based on Social Learning and Behavior Exchange Principles.* New York: Brunner/Mazel.

Jones, E., and Davis, K. E. (1965). From acts to dispositions: the attribution process in person perception. In *Advances in Experimental Social Psychology,* ed. L. Berkowitz, vol. 2: pp. 219–266. New York: Academic Press.

Kant, I. (1782/1988). *Prolegomena to Any Future Metaphysics That Can Qualify as a Science.* Trans. P. Carus. La Salle, IL: Open Court.

Kelley, H. H. (1967). Attribution theory in social psychology. In *Nebraska Symposium on Motivation,* ed. D. Levine, vol. 15: pp. 192–238. Lincoln: University of Nebraska Press.

Kelly, G. (1955). *The Psychology of Personal Constructs.* New York: Norton.

Kuhn, T. S. (1970). *The Structure of Scientific Revolutions.* Chicago: University of Chicago Press.

Langer, E. (1989). *Mindfulness.* Reading, MA: Addison-Wesley.

Layden, M. A., Newman, C. F., Freeman, A., and Morse, S. B. (1993). *Cognitive Therapy of Borderline Personality Disorder.* Needham Heights, MA: Allyn & Bacon.

Lazarus, A. (1977). *In the Mind's Eye: The Power of Imagery for Personal Enrichment.* New York: Guilford.

Lazarus, R. (1991). *Emotion and Adaptation.* New York: Oxford University Press.

Lazarus, R., and Folkman, S. (1984). *Stress, Appraisal and Coping.* New York: Springer.

Leahy, R. L. (1978). *Children's judgments of excuses.* Paper presented at meetings of the Society for Research in Child Development. April, Atlanta.

_____ (1979). The child's conception of mens rea: information mitigating punishment judgments. *Journal of Genetic Psychology* 134: 71–78.

_____ (1985). The costs of development: clinical implications. In *The Development of the Self.* Orlando, FL: Academic Press.

_____ (1991). Scripts in cognitive therapy: the systemic perspective. *Journal of Cognitive Psychotherapy: An International Quarterly* 5: 291–304.

_____ (1992a). Cognitive therapy on Wall Street: schemas and scripts of invulnerability. *Journal of Cognitive Pychotherapy: An International Quarterly* 6: 1–14.

_____ (1992b). *Development and emotion in cognitive therapy.* Paper presented at the meeting of the Association for Advancement of Behavior Therapy, Boston, November.

_____ (1993). *Strategies of resistance in cognitive therapy.* Paper presented at the meeting of the Association for the Advancement of Behavior Therapy, Atlanta, November.

_____ (1995). Cognitive development and cognitive therapy. *Journal of Cognitive Psychotherapy: An International Quarterly,* 9: 173–184.

Leahy, R. L., and Beck, A. T. (1988). Cognitive therapy of depression and mania. In *Depression and Mania,* ed. A. Georgotas and R. L. Cancro. New York: Elsevier.

Lewinsohn, P. M. (1974). A behavioral approach to depression. In *The Psychology of Depression: Contemporary Theory and Research,* ed. R. J. Friedman and M. M. Katz, pp. 157–185. New York: Wiley.

Lewinsohn, P. M., Antonuccio, D. O., Steinmetz, J. L., and Teri, L. (1984). *The Coping with Depression Course: A Psychoeducational Intervention for Unipolar Depression.* Eugene, OR: Castalia.

Lewinsohn, P. M., and Gotlib, I. H. (1995). Behavioral theory and treatment of depression. In *Handbook of Depression,* ed. E. E. Beckham and W. R. Leber. New York: Guilford.

Lewinsohn, P. M., Hoberman, H., Teri, L., and Hautzinger, M. (1985). An interpretive theory of depression. In *Theoretical Issues in Behavior Therapy,* ed. S. Reiss and R. Bootzin, pp. 331–359. New York: Academic Press.

Locke, H. J., and Wallace, K. M. (1959). Short marital-adjustment and prediction tests: their reliability and validity. *Marriage and Family Living* 21: 251–255.

Loftus, E. (1980). *Memory.* Reading, MA: Addison-Wesley.

Loftus, E., and Ketcham, K. (1995). *The Myth of Repressed Memory: False Memories and Allegations of Sexual Abuse.* New York: St. Martin's.

Lorenz, K. (1966). *On Aggression.* New York: Harcourt Brace.

Markman, H. J. (1984). The longitudinal study of couples' interactions: implications for understanding and predicting the development of marital distress. In *Marital Interaction: Analysis and Modification,* ed. K. Halweg and N. S. Jacobson, pp. 253–281. New York: Guilford.

Marks, I. M. (1987). *Fears, Phobia and Rituals: Panic, Anxiety and Their Disorders.* New York: Oxford University Press.

McNally, R. J. (1994). *Panic Disorder: A Critical Analysis.* New York: Guilford.

Meichenbaum, D. (1974). *Cognitive-Behavior Modification.* Morristown, NJ: General Learning Press.

———— (1991). Toward a cognitive theory of self-control. In *Consciousness and Self-Regulation,* ed. G. Schwartz and D. Shapiro, pp. 223–260. New York: Plenum.

Mercier, M. A. (1993). *Cognitive therapy of dysthymia.* Paper presented at the meeting of the Association for the Advancement of Behavior Therapy. November, Atlanta.

Nolen-Hoecksema, S. (1987). Sex differences in unipolar depression: evidence and theory. *Psychological Bulletin* 101: 259–282.

Novaco, R. W. (1978). Anger and coping with stress: cognitive-behavioral interventions. In *Cognitive-Behavior Therapy: Research and Applications,* ed. J. P. Foreyt and D. P. Rathjen, pp. 135–173. New York: Plenum.

Patterson, G. (1982). *Coercive Family Processes.* Eugene, OR: Castalia.

Persons, J. (1989). *Cognitive Therapy in Practice: A Case Formulation Approach.* New York: Norton.

Piaget, J. (1954). *The Construction of Reality in the Child.* New York: Basic Books.

———— (1965). *The Moral Judgment of the Child.* New York: Free Press.

———— (1970). *Genetic Epistemology.* New York: Norton.

Rehm, L. P. (1977). A self-control model of depression. *Behavior Therapy* 8: 787–804.

———— (1990). Cognitive and behavioral theories. In *Depressive Disorders: Facts, Theories and Treatment Methods,* ed. B. B. Wolman and G. Stricker, pp. 64–91. New York: Wiley.

Rosch, E. (1973). Natural categories. *Cognitive Psychology* 4:

328–350.

Salkovskis, M., and Kirk, J. (1989). Obsessional disorders. In *Cognitive Therapy for Psychiatric Problems: A Practical Guide*, ed. K. Hawton, M. Salkovskis, and J. Kirk, pp. 129–168. New York: Oxford University Press.

Seligman, M. E. P. (1975). *Helplessness.* San Francisco: W. H. Freeman.

Shapiro, D. (1965). *Neurotic Styles.* New York: Basic Books.

Skinner, B. F. (1957). *Verbal Behavior.* New York: Appleton-Century-Crofts.

Spitzer, R., Williams, J. B., Gibbon, M., and First, M. (1992). The structured clinical interview for *DSM-III-R* (SCID): history, rationale and description. *Archives of General Psychiatry* 49: 624–636.

Steketee, G. S. (1993). *Treatment of Obsessive-Compulsive Disorder.* New York: Guilford.

Stuart, R. B. (1980). *Helping Couples Change: A Social-Learning Approach to Marital Therapy.* New York: Guilford.

Sullivan, H. S. (1953). *The Interpersonal Theory of Psychiatry.* New York: Norton.

Tannen, D. (1990). *You Just Don't Understand: Women and Men in Conversation.* New York: Morrow.

Tedeschi, J. T., and Felson, R. B. (1994). *Violence, Aggression, and Coercive Actions.* Washington, DC: American Psychological Association.

Thase, M. E., and Beck, A. T. (1993). Overview of cognitive therapy. In *Cognitive Therapy with Inpatients: Developing a Cognitive Milieu*, ed. J. H. Wright, M. E. Thase, A. T. Beck, and J. W. Ludgate. New York: Guilford.

Wegner, D. M. (1989). *White Bears and Other Unwanted Thoughts: Suppression, Obsession, and the Psychology of Mental Control.* New York: Guilford.

Weiner, B. (1974). Achievement motivation as conceptualized by an attribution theorist. In *Achievement Motivation and Attribution Theory.* Morristown, NJ: General Learning Press.

_____ (1995). *Judgments of Responsibility: A Foundation for a Theory of Social Conduct.* New York: Guilford.

Wilson, E. O. (1975). *Sociobiology: The New Synthesis.* Cambridge, MA: Belknap.

Wilson, J. Q. (1993). *The Moral Sense.* New York: Free Press.

Wolpe, J. (1958). *Psychotherapy by Reciprocal Inhibition.* Stanford, CA: Stanford University Press.

Yalom, I. D. (1989). *Love's Executioner and Other Tales of Psychotherapy.* New York: Basic Books.

Young, J. E. (1990). *Cognitive Therapy for Personality Disorders: A Schema-Focused approach.* Sarasota, FL: Professional Resource Exchange.

INDEX